# LEARN ABOUT SEX

## The Contemporary Guide for Young Adults

Gary F. Kelly
Headmaster, The Clarkson School
and
Director, Student Development Center
Clarkson University
Potsdam, New York

THIRD EDITION

T 84924

## BARRON'S

Woodbury, New York • London • Toronto • Sydney

*All inquiries should be addressed to:*
Barron's Educational Series, Inc.
113 Crossways Park Drive
Woodbury, New York 11797

*Library of Congress Catalog Card No.* 86-17443
International Standard Book No. 0-8120-2432-X

**Library of Congress Cataloging-in-Publication Data**

Kelly, Gary F.
    Learning about sex.

    Includes bibliographies and index.
    1. Sex instruction for youth. I. Title.
[DNLM: 1. Sex Education.    HQ 35 K29L]
HQ35.K46    1986        612.6'007        86-17443
ISBN 0-8120-2432-X

PRINTED IN THE UNITED STATES OF AMERICA

6789  510  987654321

To my Betsy, who has enriched my life

## Acknowledgments

I would like to gratefully acknowledge the following publishers for allowing me to use material from their publications in this book:

D. Van Nostrand Company for an illustration from *Human Sexuality* by James Leslie McCary, copyright 1978 by Litton Educational Publishing, Inc. Reprinted by permission of D. Van Nostrand Company.

*Ms. Magazine* for excerpts from the Cody/Sadis marriage contract, copyright 1975 by *Ms. Magazine.* Reprinted with permission.

# Contents

# Preface

Writing this book turned out to be fun. When I was originally contacted about writing a book on sexuality, my reaction was somewhat negative. I did, however, begin to think about whatever unique features I might be able to include in such a book. I had been involved in sex education programs for teenagers for several years and had seen the kinds of materials toward which they responded positively, along with plenty of materials which were for the most part useless. In any case, I decided to try writing two sample chapters. I was happy with the results and passed the chapters along to some colleagues for their comments. They encouraged me to continue writing.

Several months passed before final contractual arrangements were complete. During that period, this book was incubating inside my head. When it started flowing out onto paper, the words came with surprising ease. The book was ready to be written, and watching each chapter take shape was exciting indeed.

This is a book which can provide accurate information about sex, as well as helping readers—particularly teenagers—clarify their needs and values relating to sex. It can be used individually or in classrooms. I sincerely hope it will be read not only by young people, but by their parents, teachers, and religious leaders.

I have been overwhelmed by the very positive reaction to the previous editions. I deeply appreciate the time which many young people and teachers have taken to write me with their kind comments and excellent suggestions for improvement. I continue to learn about human sexuality myself, and the reactions to this book have often helped me to change my own attitudes and values. I am pleased to have this opportunity to use ten more years of learning to polish *Learning About Sex* into an even better book than it was before.

A number of people have cooperated in the production and revision of the book and deserve acknowledgment. The first person to read all of the material, even before it was typed, was my wife Betsy. As my toughest editor, she eliminated much of the "junk" and helped me think through the best ways to express many concepts. I am indebted to her for her constant loving encouragement and her tolerance of my long quiet hours of writing.

Several people read portions of the original manuscript and offered their comments and suggestions. These include Mary Calderone, Derek Burleson, Lorna Brown, Fritz Renick, Ronald Gold, Jim Cerio, Bill Thickstun, Jeanne Shapiro, Bob Genn, Sheila and Maryellen Locke, and Barbara Kelly. My editor at Barron's, Carole Berglie, effected the final honing of the manuscript, and her support and cooperation have been greatly appreciated. Of course, I assume full responsibility for any inaccuracies or weaknesses which may remain.

In revising the book for this third edition, the following individuals have offered useful suggestions: Brian McNaught, Frances Campbell, Tobin Hart, Helen Hutchinson, Art Siebert, and Barbara Simpkins.

*Let Me Hear From You . . .*

I hope this book will be of use to you, regardless of your age or whether you are a student, parent, or teacher. I would be very interested in your reactions to what is written in the following pages and how it is written. Your comments and suggestions might also be useful for any future revisions of the book. So please feel free to write me a note. Although I cannot promise you a personal reply, all comments will be appreciated. Thank you for reading.

Gary F. Kelly

# Introduction

There isn't a person picking up this book who won't find something of special help and meaning in it. Let's face it—as things are today, sex becomes a problem at some time or other in everyone's life. That doesn't mean that sex *has* to be a problem. In fact, few babies are ever born into the world with a potential sex problem built into them. On the contrary, practically every baby is born with the potential for a happy, easy, confident sex life when grown up. Sex problems are acquired during the growing-up process.

By the time most children are five years old, they have acquired at least one problem: the feeling that something is seriously wrong with them for asking questions about where babies come from, or for finding pleasure in touching their own sex organs, or both!

Then in their early teens some boys will be worried that their penises are getting too big too fast, or not getting big fast enough; some girls will have exactly the same worries about their breasts; and nobody gets around to assuring them that development does not go at the same pace for everyone, but that they'll all get there in the end. In their late teens some young adults will worry about how you do it; others will worry about how to resist the pressure put on them by others *to* do it. Some will worry that they might be homosexual; others will know they are homosexual and worry that someone will find out. Still others are worried that if they have a homosexual teacher (or clergyman or doctor or friend) they might "catch" it as if it were some sort of disease. Every single one of these worries, which cause so many problems to the worriers, is absolutely unnecessary, for not one of them is based on anything but myth and ignorance.

The man who wrote this book for you (whatever your age may be) is a real friend of people. In it he stands up and tells the truth about sex, and he does so in an open, transparent, loving way that tells you he remembers well what every one of these worries feels like, and what problems they can produce. He is one of many people today who are setting forth the facts we now have about sex in order to prevent the worries and the problems. He—and I—don't believe that problems need to be part of the sexual lives of human beings, for sex was meant to be the source of only two things in life: babies, and joy between two people who are very important to each other. Procreation and recreation—both of these aspects of sex can be used by people in good or bad ways. A baby is the result of the procreative use of sex. However, with the earth getting more and more crowded, and resources getting more and more used up, procreation simply has to be thought about in the most responsible and thoughtful way—for the sake of the crowded world *and* for the sake of the baby who would have to grow up in it. To have a baby simply for one's own selfish pleasure is today immoral and shows no real concern for the ultimate good of the child nor of the adult that child will become.

Sex for recreation is quite a new thought. It means that as a relationship between two people becomes deep-rooted and intense, with increasing meaning for them both, sexual pleasure can begin to act as a source of renewal or re-creation for them. Certainly to experience another person intensely and entirely is one of the great privileges of being born a human being, and privileges impose certain responsibilities.

A book such as this could not have been written twenty years ago. Its appearance in a third edition means that we are finally learning that fear, shame, guilt and other negative attitudes about the sexual part of our lives, combined with ignorance about the facts, cause too many people to miss out on this beautiful part of living.

Therefore we should be willing to learn about sex—to understand it, to deal with it in ourselves constructively and responsibly, and to deal with the sexuality of other people in ways that help, not harm them. That's the purpose of this book, so it is not only a book for young adults; it is for all those who are involved in any way with young adults—parents, teachers, doctors, religious counselors. All of us need to understand sexuality better so that we can choose the way we will use ours in our own lives.

I hope my two great-grandsons and my great-granddaugh-
ter will get as much out of this book when they are your age as I
feel you will.

Mary S. Calderone, M.D.
Co-Founder and Former
    President
Sex Information and Education
    Council of the U.S.

# 1      From Me To You

Another book about SEX! It hardly seems that we need one, but I shall try to explain why this particular book may be a little different from some others, and why I decided to write it.

Depending on the situation, I am known by several different titles, including sex educator, sex counselor, and therapist, director of a university counseling center, and Headmaster of a school for talented high school students. Because of my involvement in these areas, I have worked with a number of local and national groups that help people understand their sexuality. It was because of these things that I was asked to write this book.

But for now, I would prefer that you forgot about my professional background because it is of secondary importance in the chapters which follow. What is most important is the fact that I am a sexual person, just as you are. We were born with biological sexuality—as male or female—but that is only the start. We also share a wide variety of sexual feelings. In the forty some years I have lived, I have often had to struggle to understand my sexuality. By that, I mean that I have often been confused, afraid, guilty, or worried about my sexual feelings and sexual behaviors. At the same time, I have gradually accepted my sexual nature as a very positive and pleasurable part of my personality and of my life.

When I was experiencing confusion and worry about sex as a young man in my teens, I often wished I could talk with someone. There seemed to be no one with whom I could share these deepest feelings, and besides I was a rather shy person anyway. So, even though I joked around with other guys about sex and seemed pretty self-assured on the surface, I was quite alone as I tried to understand who I was as a sexual person. There were many things relating to sex about which I could not fin much information, and I didn't always trust the stories which my friends had to offer. When I talk to teenagers today, I realize that things are not much different. Therefore, I decided to go ahead and write this book.

In part, this is the book I wished I could have had back then. These are the things I should have known and the things I should have though very carefully about. But I also know that many things have changed since I was a teenager. For this reason, many young people have helped me decide what areas should be discussed here. It was particularly important for me to learn what girls thought would be important to include, for it is natural that I tend to identify more with the sexual development of boys.

### Where I Stand

I do not think it possible to write a book about sex without having many of my own values, opinions, and points of view showing through. Perhaps if we just stuck to the facts about body functioning, less of myself would become a part of the discussion. But I believe it is important for every individual—young and old—to consider much more than just how his or her body functions in sexual ways. All of us must work to understand what role our sexuality is going to play in our lives: who we are as sexual people. And that means thinking and deciding about what we believe in, what kinds of people we want to be, how we are going to relate to other people, and what kinds of feelings we have. I hope that this book will help you to take a closer look at many of these things within yourself.

However, since many of my own values are going to be reflected in the pages ahead, I want you to know where I stand on many basic sexual issues. And I want you to understand that these are the values which have gradually come to have meaning and importance in *my* life. They have brought *me* happiness and satisfaction. That is not to say that they are the only "right" ways of thinking. You will have to sort through where you stand on these issues in your own way.

As you read about my values in the next few pages, you may see that you do not agree with some of them or you may realize that your parents would not agree with them. You may even decide that this is not the right book about sex for you. In any case, it is my hope that many people will keep reading and trying to decide where they stand. Even if you do not agree with an idea or value, it may be valuable to bounce it around inside and thus clarify what your own ideas or values on the subject might be.

Here are some of the values about human sexuality which are important to me.

I believe that:

1. Our sexual feelings and behaviors are an important part of our lives with the potential for great pleasure and enjoyment. To have sexual feelings and fantasies is healthy and good. However, the potential for negative effects is also present in our sexual lives and that is why decisions regarding sex should be made with careful thought.

2. Each individual must spend time discovering how sexuality is going to fit into his or her life. That means eventually understanding one's own sexual feelings, sexual behaviors, and sexual preferences. It also means that in making decisions about sex, all of us must consider the sexual values of those people who are important to us, the values we have learned from religion and education, and the values of our community and the larger society around us.

3. Each of us has a responsibility to show concern for other people who come into our lives, whether it be in a sexual encounter or any other way. Any sex which involves the exploitation or other hurting of someone surely loses some of its positive and pleasurable aspects.

4. People differ greatly in their preferences for various forms of sexual behavior. I cannot judge the "rightness" or

"wrongness" of any of these behaviors. Instead, I hope that you can find the sexual life-style which is best for your own life—one which will provide great pleasure for everyone involved; lead to happiness and satisfaction; feel natural and spontaneous; and, of special importance, a sexual life-style that helps you to feel good about the person you are.

### How Did I Get There?

Did you ever stop to think how you have come to be the person you are? Why you have the values that you do? When we are born, our values are pretty simple and are based mostly on "creature comforts": loud noises are bad; being warmly cuddled is good; being hungry is bad; having bright things to look at is good. As we grow up, the picture gets far more complicated. People around us begin to teach us many more values.

As children, when we learn those lessons from other people well, we are praised and made to feel that we are good. When we do not do so well at showing that we have those values, we are made to feel guilty and that we are not so good. In this manner, we learn a variety of ways to see ourselves and the world around us.

For me, there was also a time when I was a teenager when I began gradually to question many of those values which had been taught to me. I was no longer sure they were all so right for my life. When I expressed my doubts to my parents and teachers and a lot of other people, they sometimes would get angry with me. That would just make me more confused, and I often got angry too.

Yet, my questioning process has had to continue, and it still continues today in my life. There are still many issues and questions which are unresolved in my head. I still make mistakes. I still get confused. I still wonder and get scared about whether I am right or wrong—and lose sleep over it! I still get messed up sometimes in my dealings with other people. But for now, I accept all of this as a part of my *life*. In fact, I am beginning to think that it all just means that I am *living*—thinking, feeling, sorting, and deciding—as I go. Maybe when I think I have "gotten it all together,'' it will just mean I've died a little. So I guess I hope I never get it there completely!

### Where Do You Stand?

As I said before, I hope that one of the main uses of this book will be for you to take a close look at what you believe in. Probably on many issues, you're still thinking and wondering where you do stand. Good. I am hoping that you will take as long as you need to find the values and decisions that will feel right and good for you. Even if your mind is pretty settled on most issues, I also hope you will be open for change in the future, in case such a change would be best for your life.

For now, I would like to offer some questions about which I have discovered many young adults are thinking. I am certainly not asking you to answer the questions definitely and finally. Just see if you have thought about some of these issues and see just how clear your thinking is right now. They are purposely very open and general. Perhaps you will want to come back to these questions from time to time as you read this book and in the months ahead to see how your thoughts have changed or clarified themselves:

> To what extent do you place other people's needs ahead of or behind your own needs?
> What do you think about your own sexual feelings?
> How important is masturbation in your life?

What kinds of things are especially sexually interesting
   to you?
How far will you go with other people to get whatever
   you want?
Do you think that the only proper place for sex is in a
   marriage between a woman and man?
How do you feel about people whose sexual interests
   lie outside the traditional male-female roles?
Do you feel there is a place for sex in your life (or the
   lives of others) outside of a loving, committed relationship?
How honest are you with other people about your feelings and thoughts? How honest are you with
   yourself?
What is love to you, and what part does it play in your
   life?
Where do you stand on using various methods of birth
   control?

**Why Not Advice?**

   You will not find much advice in this book. This may disap-
point you because I've discovered that a great many people are
looking for advice on which decisions they should make. I have
also found that giving someone else advice is one of the most
dangerous things I can do, for two reasons:

   First, if I tell other people what they should or should not do,
I am assuming that I know how to live their lives better than they
do. That means that I have placed myself in a sort of superior,
all-knowing position, with all kinds of extra wisdom. The fact is,
of course, that no one really deserves such a position. Each of
us must live his or her own life, weighing decisions carefully in
an individual way. No one can do that for us.

   Secondly, if I give someone advice, I have taken over the
responsibility for that person's life. If the advice works well, then
I am to be praised, and the person who took the advice may feel
even more strongly that his or her own judgment is poor. If the
advice does not work. then it is I who should be partly blamed.
In my opinion, such a spot is not really fair to either of us. If I

care about you (and that includes respecting and trusting you), then I must *allow* you to take the responsibility for your own life. That is your right, as it is mine.

Some teenagers have said something like this to me: "But you're an adult; you've had more experience with life. You should be able to tell me what to do." My experiences are just that: *mine*. They have become a part of *my life* and *my* decision-making. Although I can share what they have meant to me—and would enjoy sharing that with you—you must remember that your life is different from mine; you have had and will have your own experiences. You will even make some of your own mistakes. That is an unavoidable part of living and growing.

It is natural, of course, for people who are close to us—our parents, brothers and sisters, friends, and others—to want us to be spared from hurt feelings, guilt, worry, and so forth. They sometimes want to prevent us from making the same kinds of mistakes or poor decisions that they feel have been a part of their own lives. So you will get plenty of advice from plenty of people. Use it: listen carefully, consider the quality of the person's life who is offering the advice, weigh it, think and feel about it, examine it with the knowledge of who you are and what you want from *your* life. I hope you will not accept it blindly.

### In the Pages Ahead
One of the main purposes of this book is to help you take a better look at yourself as a sexual person. That will mean learning more about the sex organs of your body and the ways in which they function. But that is only a part of the total picture. To understand your sexuality more completely, you will also need to take a closer look at your emotions or feelings and at your attitudes toward relationships with other people. It will also be important for you to learn more about the sex organs of other people, including those of the opposite sex. This book can help you accomplish all of these things.

The chapters ahead would not be very complete if we did not take some pages to discuss femininity and masculinity: what does it mean to be a woman or a man in today's society? How are you becoming a man or a woman? What do you expect of yourself and other men and women?

I have not tried to pull any punches in this book. I want to be honest and frank with you as you read on and learn more about sex. Nothing is meant to embarrass you or to make you uncomfortable.

In describing the parts of the body and sexual activities, I have used the "accepted" terms. In parentheses, you will often find some common slang words which are also used by many people. More slang words are given in the Appendix in *Four-letter and Other Words*. If you are uncertain of the pronunciation of any of the words, also consult the Appendix (page 180). Of course, you will have to decide which words you will want to use in various situations. It may be important to keep in mind that some words are offensive to some individuals. You may want to be considerate of their sensitivities. It may be particularly useful to learn the more socially acceptable terms so that you will be able to communicate with doctors, nurses, lawyers, or trusted adults who could help you in special situations.

Remember—as the reader of this book, you are in control of it. You may decide which areas you wish to concentrate on and which you wish to skip over or disagree with. I shall try to share my ideas as warmly as I can, and I hope that you will try to believe that I really do care about *you* as an individual and about your growth as a sexual person.

**For Further Reading**

Bell, Ruth. *Changing Bodies, Changing Lives: A Book for Teens on Sex and Relationships*. New York: Random House, 1980.

Eagan, Andrea B. *Why am I so Miserable if These are the Best Years of My Life?* (Revised). New York: Avon Books, 1979.

Gordon, Sol. *Psychology for You*. Fayetteville, NY (P.O. Box 583): Ed-U-Press, 1981.

Gordon, Sol. *The Teenage Survival Book*. Fayetteville, NY: Ed-U-Press, 1981.

Hettlinger, Richard. *Your Sexual Freedom: Letters to Students*. New York: Continuum Publishing, 1982.

Johnson, Eric W. and Johnson, Corrine. *Love and Sex and Growing Up*. New York: Bantam, 1979.

# 2     Growing As a Sexual Person

Think for a moment how your body looked when you were five or six years old. Sometime soon, you might even try to dig out some old photographs or home movies of yourself back then. Perhaps you can find a picture of yourself in a swimsuit or maybe even with nothing on. What was your body like then?

Chances are your body was mostly straight up and down—not many curves or bulges. It was also probably quite smooth, with the soft skin of a child and very little hair anywhere except on your head.

Think of how your body looks now. You probably often have a chance to see your naked body in a mirror. Sometime when you have the privacy you need, take a good close look at your body and think about the changes that have happened to it since you were five or six. What kinds of changes have occurred in you and how far along you are with the changes depend on your age, your rate of development, your sex, the characteristics you have inherited from your parents, and a variety of other factors. The chances are that you are "normal," regardless of what your body is like now. More about that as we go along.

Your growth and development are continuous throughout your lifetime. However, scientists who study human growth and development often find it convenient to divide the human life cycle into important events and stages such as: Birth, Infancy, Childhood, Puberty, Adolescence, Adulthood, Old Age, and Death. Regardless of which part of the life cycle you are now living, you are, always have been, and always will be a sexual person. You may even remember the sexual feelings of your younger years and the curiosity you had concerning your sex organs. Your sexual feelings may be stronger now, and your curiosity may well be growing along with your sex organs. I am still very curious about my body, how it functions, and how it can give me pleasure.

*Puberty* is defined as that time in your life when your sex organs become capable of reproduction—producing another human being. That can be at different ages for different people, but it is usually between the ages of nine and thirteen. It generally happens a little later for boys than for girls. There are many physical changes which occur in your body around the time of puberty which will be discussed soon. Once your body has reached puberty, you are considered to be an *adolescent*. The period of *adolescence* refers to that time when you are learning to be an adult. Many of us talk about adulthood, but few of us seem to understand fully what that means. Perhaps by the time you finish this book, you will know a bit more about what you think being an adult is all about. In any case, I never liked being labeled an "adolescent," so I shall avoid using that term in this book. You are a person, and this book can be useful to you at whatever age you wish to read it.

In the next few sections of this chapter, the changes of the male and female bodies are described, with special emphasis on the sex organs. I suggest that you read all of these sections thoroughly so that you get better acquainted with your own body as well as gain a fuller understanding of the bodies of others.

### If You Are a Male . . .

You have probably looked your body over carefully many times, and you may have seen the bodies of other boys (Figure 2.1). There have certainly been some changes since you were five years old. I shall describe some of the changes which have probably already happened or which may happen to you soon.

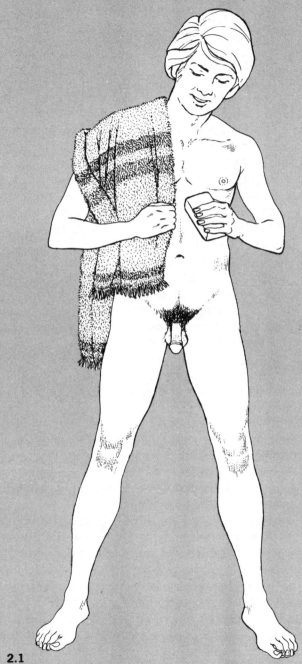

Figure 2.1

Looking at the drawings and diagrams in this chapter may help you to understand what is being discussed.

For one thing, you have grown taller. Around puberty, boys and girls go through several months of very rapid growth. Boys' shoulders begin to widen as they grow taller. Most boys have attained 98% of their final height by the age of 18. There is also a gradual increase in the amount of hair on the body. Darker, coarser hair appears under the arms, in the *pubic* area above and around your sex organs, and, eventually, on the arms, legs, chest, and face. How much hair you will have, what color it is, and where it is distributed depend mostly on characteristics you have inherited from your parents.

Another change you may have noticed is a deepening of the voice. As the larynx, or voicebox, grows longer, the voice deepens. During the period when a boy's voice is changing, there may be some squeaking and cracking in the voice that some boys find embarrassing. Girls' voices become lower pitched also, but generally not as low as boys'.

If you are a male, perhaps you have been especially curious about the changes which occur in your sex organs. Particularly noticeable is the increase in size of the *penis* (cock, prick, dick) and the *testes* (balls, nuts). The penis becomes somewhat longer and thicker around the time of puberty and after. The two testes are located inside a pouch of skin called the *scrotum* (bag) or *scrotal sac*. Sometimes, the testes and scrotum are referred to as *testicles*. You will be able to feel that the testes are larger and heavier and that they may be moved around slightly inside the scrotum.

In the next few years, it will be important for you to learn how to examine your testes occasionally to check for any unusual lumps or bumps. The best time to do this is after a hot shower or bath, when the testes are hanging down from the body. Simply roll each testis between your fingers, and if you discover a small hard lump directly on the testis, report it to your doctor. You will feel tubes and other structures above the testes inside the scrotum, but these belong there. Lumps on the testes are not common, and may not be something to be very concerned about. However, if a lump is discovered, consult your doctor.

The skin of the penis and scrotum becomes darker as males grow and develop, and hair appears on the scrotum and base of the penis. As the testes get larger, the scrotal skin becomes somewhat wrinkled and has small nubs at the bases of the hairs. You probably have noticed that one testis hangs slightly lower than the other. This is true for most boys and men, and apparently has no particular significance.

The penis is a cylindrical shaft of tissues with a smooth, highly sensitive "head" or *glans*. When a boy is born, the head of the penis is covered by a fold of skin called the *foreskin* or prepuce. Sometimes, because of family tradition or religious custom, most of the foreskin is removed by a simple surgical procedure called *circumcision*. This is most often done just after birth at the parents' request, before the baby boy is brought home from the hospital. It can be done, however, at any age if a doctor feels that it would be advisable.

If your penis is circumcised, you can see the head of the penis easily (Figure 2.2). With an uncircumcised penis, the foreskin must be pulled back for the head to be seen. Boys who are not circumcised should pull back the foreskin and wash the head of the penis often to prevent odor or mild infections from developing. The functioning of the penis seems to be the same

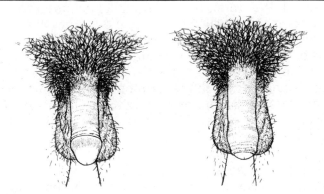

**Figure 2.2**  A circumcised penis (left) and an uncircumcised penis (right).

whether or not it is circumcised. Recently, there has been controversy over whether circumcision should be performed routinely. Opponents insist that it provides no particular health benefits. It is more common in North America than in European societies.

Boys and men often worry about the size or shape of their penises and wonder if they are "normal" or not. In our society, it often seems that people believe the myth that the size of a man's penis has something to do with "how much of a man" he is. There is no truth to that belief at all. The size and shape of one's penis seems to be primarily the result of heredity. Typically, the limp penis is between two and four inches in length after puberty, but normal boys and men may have penises smaller or larger than that. The shaft and head of the penis are found in a wide variety of widths and shapes, from thin and quite pointed to thick and very rounded. Some penises have a slight curve toward one side. Blood vessels are often visible beneath the skin of the penis.

Boys usually notice during childhood that their penises sometimes get stiffer and longer. This is called an *erection* (hard-on, boner). As you have probably already realized, erections happen when a boy becomes sexually excited or aroused. The ridge around the head of the penis is particularly sensitive, and stimulation of this ridge quickly leads to sexual excitement and erection. There are a great many other things that can cause an erection, many of which have nothing to do with sex. Sometimes, for example, boys get erections when they are a little nervous or when they have to urinate badly.

Erection is the result of special nerve messages from the brain and spinal cord which cause blood to build up in the penis. There are three cylinders of spongy tissue in the shaft of the penis which become filled with blood. This causes it to become harder, thicker, and longer as it stands up and out from the body (Figure 2.3). When fully erect, most boys' penises are between five and six-and-a-half inches in length, although lengths considerably smaller and larger than those are perfectly normal as well. You may have noticed that the shaft of the erect penis is somewhat triangular in shape because of the three cylinders

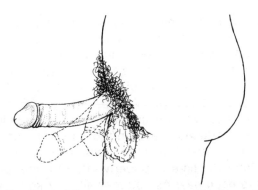

**Figure 2.3** Erection of the penis. Because of build-up blood within the spongy tissues of the penis, it becomes longer, thicker, and harder, standing up and out from the body.

of spongy tissue inside. There is no bone inside the penis, as some people believe.

Erection occurs in most forms of sexual activity, including the insertion of the penis into the female's body during *sexual intercourse* (making love, fucking, screwing). However, there are many forms of pleasurable bodily sharing in which erection need not take place.

### Male Sex Organs

Now we may discuss the male sex organs and their functions in more detail. It will help if you locate the organs on Figure 2.4. We shall begin with the testes.

Before a boy is born, his testes are located inside his body. A few weeks before birth, the testes descend through a special tube (inguinal canal) into the scrotum. In a few boys, one or both of the testes may not come out into the scrotum, and sometimes medical attention is required during childhood to remedy the situation. As a boy reaches puberty, his testes have two very important functions:

1) To produce special chemicals called *hormones* which help control his growth and development as a man, including the body changes just discussed and his sexual feelings.

2) To produce the tiny, swimming units called *sperm* which are necessary for reproduction. Each sperm has a head and a tail which moves it along (Figure 2.5). Sperm are so tiny that 120 million of them can be swimming in a small drop (1 ml) of fluid. They may only be observed through a microscope.

Each testis has within it tiny, tightly coiled tubules in which the sperm are produced. Laid end-to-end, the tubules from a single testis would stretch several hundred feet. The testes produce sperm from the time of puberty into old age, probably 500 million or more *each day!* As you may already know, the temperature of the human body is normally about 98.6° F. or 37° C. Sperm are best produced at temperatures three or four degrees lower than body temperature. This is the reason why the location of the testes in a special scrotal pouch is so ideal. The scrotum is supported by special muscles which can draw the testes up

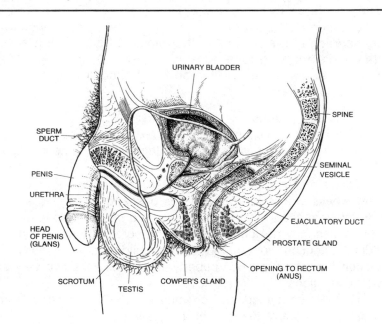

**Figure 2.4**   Sex and reproductive organs of the male: external and internal, side view.

closer to the body or lower them farther away, thus regulating their temperature. For example, boys usually notice that when they are swimming or showering in cold water, their testes are tight up against their bodies. This keeps them warmer. In hotter surroundings, the testes are lowered away from the body to keep them slightly cooler.

In the head of each sperm is a set of twenty-three chromosomes, containing the genes that can pass characteristics on to our children. One of the functions of the male sex organs, then, is to transfer sperm to the female's body so that reproduction can take place. Chapter ten includes further information on human reproduction. We can now trace the pathway of the sperm to the outside of the body.

After the sperm are produced inside the tubules of the testes, they are slowly moved into other larger tubes where they may mature and grow for up to six weeks. During this time, the

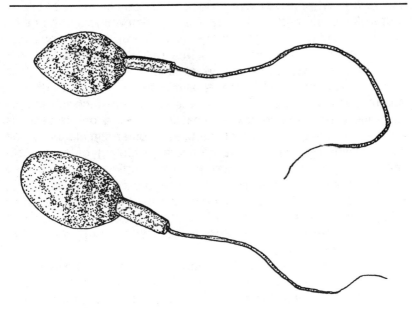

**Figure 2.5** Two typical sperm produced by the testes of a human male, magnified here about 1500 times.

weaker sperm die and are absorbed by the linings of the tubes. Gradually, the remaining sperm are moved along through a duct which is about eighteen inches in length. There is one *sperm duct,* or vas deferens, from each testis, which conducts sperm up into the body to a *seminal vesicle.* The seminal vesicles produce a chemical that activates the tails of the sperm.

There are three glands that play a part in the safe passage of sperm to the outside of the body. One of these is the *prostate gland,* located just below the urinary bladder where urine is stored. The prostate produces fluids with which the sperm will be mixed before leaving the body. The mixture is a milky-white, sticky liquid called *semen.* There are two glands, each about the size of a pea, located below the prostate gland. These *Cowper's glands* sometimes produce a fluid when a male is sexually excited. It is a clear, sticky liquid that lines the tube in the penis through which the sperm will leave the body. This tube is called the *urethra.* When a boy is or has recently been sexually excited, drops of this clear liquid may appear in the opening at the end of his penis. It is an alkaline substance which apparently neutralizes the acidity within the urethra, thus protecting the sperm.

The penis has some important functions for the body. It is through its urethra that urine is eliminated from the body and sperm eventually leave the body. It is an organ which is capable of giving males intense sexual pleasure. When a boy is sexually excited and his penis is erect, rubbing or other stimulation of the penis eventually leads to the pleasurable feeling of sexual climax or *orgasm,* accompanied by the spurting out of semen through the penis. This spurting is called *ejaculation* (coming). There are special muscles in the body near the seminal vesicles which cause the semen to be ejaculated. Special muscles close off the bladder so that urine does not pass through the urethra during sexual activity.

At the time of ejaculation, the semen may just ooze out of the penis or spurt out with some force. How much semen is produced and with what force it is ejaculated depend on many factors, including the degree of sexual excitement and the amount of stimulation. The amount of semen may vary from a few drops to a teaspoon full or more. Before a boy's body begins making sperm and semen, it is possible for him to experience the pleasurable feeling of orgasm but no liquid is ejaculated. At various times in their lives, most boys occasionally experience orgasm and ejaculation while they are asleep. This is known as a *wet dream* or *nocturnal emission*. A wet dream can be surprising, even frightening, unless the boy is aware that it is a normal, healthy body activity.

Most boys know how sexual excitement makes them feel. There often is an intense desire to experience orgasm and ejaculation. Boys usually discover from their friends or through experimentation that by rubbing the penis—usually with the hands—orgasm can be produced. This is called *masturbation* (jerking off, jacking off, whacking off, beating off). There is a whole section on masturbation in Chapter Three, pages 44–46. Be sure to read it. Orgasm is also part of the sexual pleasure which can be shared in close relationships with other people. There is more about sexual sharing throughout this book, particularly in Chapters Three, Four, and Five.

### If You Are a Female . . .

You too have probably noticed some changes in your body, and in the bodies of other girls (Figure 2.6). Consult the drawings and diagrams in this section carefully and consider your own body. They can help you to understand some of what it means physically to be a girl and a woman.

Since you were five or six years old, you have grown taller. The period of rapid growth for many girls takes place a year or two earlier than for boys of the same age. Therefore, girls around the ages of ten or eleven often find themselves maturing physically before the boys in their age group. This is sometimes embarrassing for a young woman—and for the boys—but perfectly normal. By the age of seventeen, most girls have attained 98% of their final height. As her body is getting taller, there is a widening of the pelvic or hip region. This widening may be of great importance in later life because a roomier area is being developed in which a baby may grow and develop before birth.

Pads of fat begin to develop under the skin in certain areas of the female's body as she matures, particularly on the hips, buttocks, and breasts. This results in the curvier body form of most women, as compared to the straighter body lines typical of men. At puberty, a girl's breasts also enlarge because of the addition of glandular tissue inside. When a woman gives birth to a baby, the glands in the breast will produce milk which can be fed to the baby through the nipple. Milk is generally not produced by the breasts except in late pregnancy and during the months after birth when the baby is nursing. As the breasts grow larger, so do the nipples and the darker area surrounding the nipple, called the *areola.*

Girls often have concerns and worries over the size and shape of their breasts or the color and shape of the nipples. The size of the breasts has nothing to do with "how much of a woman" she is, nor whether she will be able to breastfeed babies. Advertisers have capitalized on the anxieties of girls and women, offering a variety of exercise programs, bras and other equipment for making the breasts appear larger or "perfectly" shaped. In fact, breasts occur in a wide variety of sizes, shapes, and colors, all perfectly normal and healthy. Women should learn from a physician or nurse how to check their own breasts monthly for lumps, a valuable way to discover tumors which might indicate the presence of breast cancer.

The amount of hair on a girl's body increases also. Darker, coarser hair appears under the arms and in the *pubic* area around the external sex organs. Girls usually develop hair on their arms and legs, which some prefer to bleach or to remove by shaving or by using a hair-removing chemical cream. Our culture has created concern over bodily hair on females. Some girls are disturbed to have hairs appear on their faces, especially on the upper lip or chin. If temporary removal of these hairs through shaving or creams is unsatisfactory, a process called electrolysis can remove them for a longer period. A cosmetologist who has had special training in electrolysis must be consulted.

The changes in boys' sex organs are usually noticed more because their organs are easily observed. Nevertheless, important changes also occur in the external and internal sex organs of girls. All of their organs grow larger too.

Figure 2.6

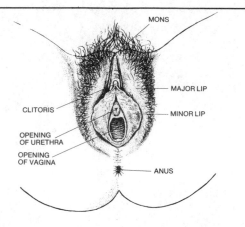

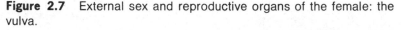

**Figure 2.7**   External sex and reproductive organs of the female: the vulva.

A girl's external sex organs located between her legs are collectively called the *vulva* (Figure 2.7). Just above the opening between the two outer folds of skin in the vulva is a slightly rounded, padded area which becomes covered with hair as the girl enters puberty. This small "mound" of tissue is termed the *mons* (or *mons Veneris; mons pubis*). It is an area where the skin has many nerve endings and is therefore capable of adding to sexual excitement when rubbed or pressed.

The two folds of skin below the mons are called the major lips (or *labia majora*). These are sensitive structures also, and they serve as protective covers for the organs they enclose. If the major lips are parted, two smaller folds of skin are visible inside. These are the minor lips (or *labia minora*). They are highly sensitive to stimulation. During sexual excitement, the minor lips may flare out somewhat, showing the inner structures more clearly.

At the point where the two minor lips come together at the top, the *clitoris* is located. This is a small cylinder of tissue with a sensitive head or *glans*. Usually only the head of the clitoris is visible, while its shaft is covered by the upper folds of the minor lips. Although the entire clitoris is usually less than an inch in length, it may be considerably longer than an inch. It does not hang freely, but is attached along its underside. It contains two cylinders of spongy tissue inside and with stimulation it becomes erect—longer, thicker, and harder. The clitoris is the most sexually excitable part of a girl's body.

Beneath the clitoris and between the minor lips, the opening of the urethra is visible. It is quite small and difficult to see. Urine passes from the bladder through the urethra and then leaves the body through this opening. Beneath the urethral opening is the opening to the vagina. The *vagina* (box, cunt, snatch, pussy) is a muscular tube about three to four inches in length. It is capable of opening up when something is inserted into it, and during sexual excitement, it deepens slightly. The vagina can be a part of a variety of sexual activities, including receiving the erect male penis during *sexual intercourse* (making love, fucking, screwing). More about that in Chapters three and five.

In many girls, some tissue called the *hymen* (cherry, maidenhead) partially covers the opening to the vagina. Hymens are observed in a variety of different shapes, some of which are shown in Figure 2.8. The hymen may be ruptured in many different ways. Sometimes, the hymen is broken by the penis during the first sexual intercourse. Insertion of other things (such as tampons) into the vagina or strenuous exercise may also break

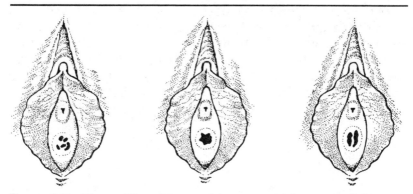

**Figure 2.8**   Three different types of hymens which may partially cover the opening of a girl's vagina.

the hymen. When the hymen is first ruptured, there may be some slight pain and bleeding. This may be prevented by having a physician cut the tissue ahead of time, using a mild local anesthetic.

In many cultures, the presence of the intact hymen has been a sign that the girl is a *virgin,* a person who has never had sexual intercourse. This is obviously not a reliable sign, since the hymen may be ruptured by other means, or—in the case of a particularly flexible hymen—it may not be broken during intercourse at all. Therefore, the presence or absence of a hymen signifies nothing.

Many girls and women discover that pleasurable feelings may be produced by rubbing areas in the vulva with the hands or stimulating the sex organs in other ways. Sexually stimulating oneself is called *masturbation* (rubbing off, fingering), discussed more completely in Chapter Three, pages 44–46. Be certain to read that section. After a certain time of such stimulation, the pleasurable release of sexual climax or *orgasm* may be reached. Orgasm is also part of the sexual pleasure which can be shared with other people. To read more about sexual sharing, see especially Chapters Three, Four, and Five.

One of the most important signs that a girl has reached puberty is the beginning of *menstruation* (having her "period"). This involves the loss of some fluid, mixed with a small amount of blood, through the vagina about once a month. The first time this happens, a girl may be surprised or frightened unless she has been fully informed about why menstruation occurs and that it is a normal, healthy function of the female body. In the following two sections, we shall discuss a girl's sex and reproductive organs in more detail, including the importance of the menstrual cycle in human reproduction. Menstruation is only a part of that cycle.

### Inner Sex Organs of the Female

We have already explored the external sex organs of a girl. You will recall that inside the minor lips, in the area of the vulva, there was an opening to the vagina. By examining Figure 2.9 you will note that the vagina leads upward into the body to the *uterus,* or womb, inside of which a baby can develop. Near the uterus,

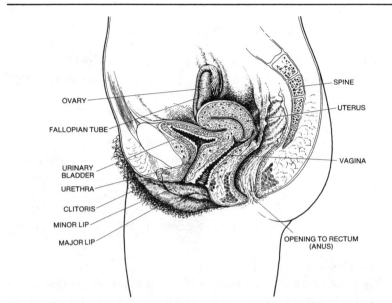

**Figure 2.9** Sex and reproductive organs of the female: external and internal, side view.

there are two ovaries, each having a narrow *fallopian tube* which leads to the uterus. These organs are essential to human reproduction.

Each ovary is about an inch in length. As a girl reaches puberty, her two ovaries have two very important functions:

1) To produce hormones which help control her growth and development as a woman, including the body changes just discussed and her sexual feelings. These special chemical substances also help control the menstrual cycle.

2) To produce the tiny *eggs,* or *ova,* necessary for reproduction. The ova produced by human females are about 1/175 inch in diameter, much larger than the male's sperm. It is when a sperm from a male joins with the female's ovum that a new human being begins to develop (also see Chapter ten).

At puberty, each ovary contains about 10,000 tiny cells which can become eggs. During a woman's lifetime, only 400 to 500 of them will actually "ripen" to become ova and then be released from the ovaries. The fallopian tubes, sometimes called *oviducts,* carry the ova which are released to the uterus, a journey of about four inches which takes about two days.

The uterus is about the size of a doubled fist and has somewhat the shape of a pear. It has very thick, muscular walls and a hollow interior. The tip of the uterus which opens into the vagina is called the *cervix*. The uterus is sometimes a site of cancer in women, and a Pap Test—described on page 173—can detect trouble before it gets serious. The Pap Test should be a part of an annual physical examination for all women. Figure 2.10 will help you understand the relative position of these organs and their activities as you read on.

### The Menstrual Cycle

If you can now identify the internal organs of the woman, you should be able to understand the changes that they undergo each month—the menstrual cycle. This cycle begins at puberty (usually between the ages of nine and fifteen), and generally continues until the woman is in her middle to late forties. When a

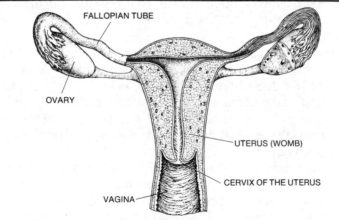

FALLOPIAN TUBE

OVARY

UTERUS (WOMB)

CERVIX OF THE UTERUS

VAGINA

**Figure 2.10**   The female reproductive system: front view, isolated from the body.

woman then ceases to menstruate, she is said to have experienced menopause. Some people refer to this time as her "change of life," although really not very much else changes. During the years before menstruation has begun and after it has ended, the female is unable to bear children. The number of days in one complete menstrual cycle varies with different individuals. For teenaged girls, it is most often thirty or thirty-one days in length. As girls enter their twenties, the amount of time often decreases, so that the average menstrual cycle takes about twenty-eight days. What actually happens is that the ovaries and uterus prepare for pregnancy each month. If pregnancy does not occur, the prepared areas are shed from the body, and the cycle starts all over again. The main stages of the cycle are described below.

1. In one of the ovaries, one of the eggs ripens and becomes larger, ready to produce a new human being if it is joined by a male sperm. In the meantime, there is a thickening of the inner lining of the uterus. Blood and other materials begin to build up in the lining so that if a developing baby, or *fetus,* is to grow there, it will have a nourishing environment to keep it alive.

2. As the uterine lining continues to thicken and prepare for pregnancy, the ovum (egg) breaks through the outer wall of the ovary. This release of the egg is called *ovulation.*

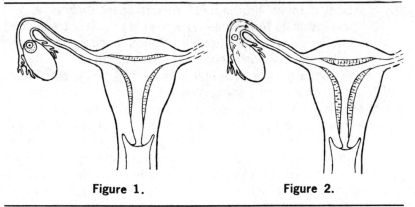

**Figure 1.**                              **Figure 2.**

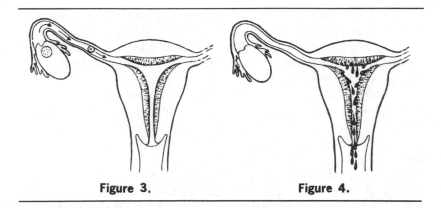

**Figure 3.**                    **Figure 4.**

3.  The egg is released into the fallopian tube, which is lined
    with microscopic hairlike projections called cilia. These
    move the ovum along toward the uterus for about two days.
    If the egg is to develop into a fetus, it must be joined by a
    sperm while it is in the tube. As the ovum moves along, the
    uterus becomes especially ready to nourish a fetus. Its lin-
    ings are very thickened and filled with blood.
    4.  If the egg does not meet with the sperm by the time it
        reaches the uterus, it apparently disintegrates. Then, the
        extra material which has thickened the lining of the uterus
        is no longer needed, and it gradually begins to deteri-
        orate. Eventually, some of this fluid and blood leaves the
        body through the vagina. This is menstruation, and it
        usually lasts from three to seven days. The cycle then
        continues, with the ripening of another egg and another
        build-up of nourishment in the uterine lining.
    As the extra lining of the uterus is deteriorating, particularly
just before menstruation, some girls and women experience unpleasant symptoms. These can include fatigue, headaches, abdominal cramps, tenderness in the breasts, an increase in pimples, and moodiness. In women where these symptoms are quite
strong, the condition is called premenstrual syndrome, or PMS
for short. Some women are able to tolerate the symptoms better
than others. Medications of various sorts may be prescribed by
a physician to prevent or relieve more severe complaints.

The fluid and blood which flow out of the vagina during menstruation must be absorbed in some way so that clothing will not be stained. There are three types of absorbent aids which girls may purchase. One is an absorbent pad or *sanitary napkin* which is placed over the vaginal opening. These napkins come in a variety of sizes and absorbencies to suit the needs of different girls. The pads are held in place by a strip of adhesive that sticks to the underpants. Another aid which many girls find convenient and easy to use is the *tampon*. This is a cylinder of absorbent material which is inserted directly into the vagina. Tampons generally do not cause discomfort, and they do not in any way stretch or damage the vagina. If a girl has difficulty inserting tampons because of her hymen, she should start with a small sized type, slowly widening the opening of the hymen. Tampons should be changed frequently so that bacteria do not build up on them in the vagina. This can cause infections, including a very serious illness called toxic shock syndrome. The printed instructions included with tampon packages give specific advice on prevention of this infection.

Despite the myths of former times, physicians seem to agree that girls and women need not limit any of their activities while they are menstruating. There is no harm at all in bathing and showering, shampooing the hair, swimming, being physically active in sports, engaging in sexual activity, or doing anything else during menstruation. Girls should avoid using menstruation as an excuse for not participating in everyday activities unless a physician has advised them of some special condition about which they should be cautious.

In learning more about human reproduction, described in more detail in Chapter ten, it is important to understand the menstrual cycle. There is further information about the cycle in that chapter.

### Growth and Growing
We have dealt with some of the major physical changes which occur as we grow toward adulthood, especially the changes in our sex organs. For most of us, our physical growth is unavoidable. With a reasonably balanced diet, protection

from the elements, and freedom from serious disease, the human body developes and grows older in a continual state of balanced change.

Think of the people in your life whom you have known for several years. Think of how they have changed. They have grown older and their bodies have changed in a variety of ways, just as yours has. But there is more to living than just growing older. We grow inside, too. It is easy to see others and ourselves growing older, but quite a different matter to get in touch with the inner growth which is also happening. Yet, to live fully and happily, it is necessary to keep in touch with that growth as closely as possible.

One of the most important areas of inner growth is our *emotions*. As most people enter their teenage years, they are beginning to get in touch with more intense feelings than they knew in childhood. They may begin having strong loving feelings for other individuals, and these loving feelings not only bring pleasure, but confusion and hurt as well. They may begin feeling depression, guilt, boredom, and fear more than when they were children. They may also feel new joys and satisfactions in their lives. Getting acquainted with all of these new intensities of feeling is part of what inner growing is all about. It is important to realize also that even when an emotion is not very pleasant, it still may be worth feeling. It may be a part of our growth as a person. We often learn to escape from our "bad" feelings as quickly as possible, when there may be real value in allowing ourselves to feel them for awhile.

Another part of our inner growth is understanding our relationships with other people. Our attitudes toward many things may change with time, if we allow ourselves to be open to such change. We need always to keep in touch with what kinds of responsibilities we feel toward others and the extent to which we need other people in our lives. Whenever we set our minds on opinions or values which *cannot* be changed no matter what, we have stifled our own growth.

### Emerging Sexual Feelings
Children often have sexual feelings and can even experience

orgasm. At puberty and during our teenage years, most of us experience our sexual feelings with greater intensity. In thinking about what I would write in this section, I realized how difficult it is to describe sexual feelings. For the most part, they can only be understood when they are felt. The term "sex drive" is often used to describe our desire for sexual stimulation and release. Sometime in late childhood and as we grow toward adulthood, there is usually an increase in this desire, which may be partly the result of increased amounts of sex hormones produced by the testes and ovaries.

At first, the deepening interest in sex may produce a vague inner tension, a longing for something which is not clearly defined. Eventually—and this occurs at different ages and rates for different individuals—the sensations become more definitely located in our sex organs. It becomes a longing or a need for stimulation of these organs. Sometimes, this longing is referred to in slang as being "horny."

There are differences among people in their degree of interest in sex. For example, some boys and girls become sexually aroused very easily and desire orgasm often. Teenagers often feel these needs rather intensely. On the other hand, some young people do not find themselves particularly interested in sex. These differences are perfectly normal.

As people grow older and go through different periods of their lives, there may be changes in the intensity of their sexual interests, and those changes may occur in either direction. In old age, there may be some gradual decline in the desire for sexual release. That does not mean, however, that older people enjoy their sexual feelings and activities any less.

It has traditionally been believed that boys have a stronger desire for sexual activity than girls, and research has shown that boys in general seem to have more frequent orgasms during their teenage years than girls. There are, of course, many individual exceptions to these statistical trends.

There is disagreement among professionals as to how much of our sexual interest is due to physical causes in our bodies and how much is due to learning. For example, some say that any differences in sexual interest between teenaged boys and girls is attributable to organic differences. Others insist that boys are simply encouraged more to explore their sexual feelings at earlier ages, while most girls are not. Perhaps if such differences really do exist, they are explainable as a combined result of organic factors *and* learning. Only further investigation will clarify the answer. The important thing is to become comfortable with whatever degree of sexual interest that seems to be a part of your personality.

As we "awaken" more fully to our sexual feelings, we often begin to feel some guilt. Hopefully, as you read through this book, your increased understanding of your own sexual feelings will help to lessen unnecessary guilt for your life. The cycles of our sexual responses are explained more fully in the next chapter.

**Time Out**

Sometime soon, try to take time for the following activities. I have suggested them to many young people, and they often report back that the exercises helped to put them in touch with themselves and their inner growth.

1. *Body Awareness*

   Find a comfortable and quiet place where you can relax. Close your eyes, and allow your hands to move lightly over your face. Touch and *really feel* your eyelids, nose, lips, ears, and neck. Pay attention to the warmth and texture of your skin. Blow your warm breath on your hands and feel the warmth. Move your fingers slowly through your hair, noting its texture and "feel." Try to become aware of the rest of your body also. Where do you feel tension? What are the areas of your body which feel the pressure of touch?

2. *Alone Time*

   We live in hectic times. It always seems there is something to do or somewhere to go, leaving very little time for ourselves. I would like you to set aside some time just to be by yourself. An hour or more would be best. If you have brothers or sisters who are noisy .or always around, go for a walk outdoors. Most important of all, spend this time *thinking about yourself* and *letting yourself have inner feelings*. If you get around to thinking about your sexuality, you might want to consider the following questions:

a) How does your body seem to compare with the bodies of others your own age?

b) What things about your body are you most satisfied with? Most dissatisfied with?

c) Have you had any worries about your sex organs or sexual activity lately? Think them through and consider seeking out someone else to talk with. (See Chapter Six)

d) Does your interest in sex seem much stronger than it used to be? Most people sometimes worry that they are thinking about sex too much, even though their great interest in sex is perfectly normal. Have you been worrying about that?

3. *Sharing*

If you have a friend whom you trust and can talk to, perhaps you could try discussing some of the above questions with him or her. The friend may then be willing to share some thoughts and concerns with you. Don't be upset, however, by differing points of view. Perhaps they will just make you think.

**For Further Reading**

Betancourt, Jeanne. *Am I Normal? An Illustrated Guide to Your Changing Body* (for Boys). New York: Avon Books, 1983.

Betancourt, Jeanne. *Dear Diary: An Illustrated Guide to Your Changing Body* (for Girls). New York: Avon Books, 1983.

Calderone, Mary S. and Johnson, Eric, W. *The Family Book About Sexuality.* New York: Harper and Row, 1981.

Gardner-Loulan, Jo Ann; Lopez, Bonnie and Quackenbush, Marcia. *Period* (Revised).San Francisco:Volcano Press,1981.

Gordon, Sol. *Facts About Sex for Today's Youth.* Fayetteville, NY (P.O. Box 583): Ed-U-Press, 1983.

McCoy, Kathy. *The Teenage Body Book Guide to Sexuality.* New York: Simon and Schuster, 1983.

Pomeroy, Wardell. *Boys and Sex.* New York: Delacorte Press, 1981.

Pomeroy, Wardell. *Girls and Sex.* New York: Delacorte Press, 1981.

## 3    Finding Your Sexuality

The last chapter dealt mostly with the physical part of our sexuality—the sex organs. I keep trying to emphasize that there is much more to your sexuality than just your sex organs. This chapter will begin to explore the changing concepts of femininity and masculinity, and it will discuss in more detail how our bodies respond sexually. These are important considerations in understanding your own sexuality.

### Becoming Women and Men

For many years, the roles which were expected of men and women in our society were very rigid. Table I summarizes some of the stereotyped views of men and women that persist even today. Some people still hold tightly to these stereotypes, while others are adopting a more flexible viewpoint.

## TABLE I
## THE TRADITIONAL STEREOTYPES OF WOMEN AND MEN

| WOMEN | MEN |
|---|---|
| Emotional and flighty; cry often and worry easily | Unemotional and stable; control their feelings and worries |
| Delicate and somewhat physically weak; tire easily and cannot stand prolonged physical exertion | Muscular and strong; have much stamina to withstand physical exertion |
| Content with household tasks such as cooking, cleaning, sewing, and caring for children | Enjoy the pressures and demands of business and earning money |
| Shy and retiring | Aggressive and forward-moving |
| Should not become sexually involved unless married | Expected to become active sexually at an earlier age and to "sow a few wild oats" |
| Tender and caring for children and others more helpless than themselves | Tend to be colder and less tolerant toward children and others |
| Quite easily swayed by the suggestions of others; tend to be followers | More independent and level-headed; not easily swayed by others; tend toward leadership |
| Have less self-confidence and self-esteem | Confident and proud; stand up for themselves |
| Concerned with people and their feelings | Concerned with impersonal objects and mechanical gadgets |
| Argue about petty matters; enjoy gossip with other women | Concentrate on important issues of politics and society; do not gossip |
| Are not expected to initiate sexual experiences | Are expected to be aggressive sexually and initiate sexual contact |
| Become sexually aroused only by the romantic and loving aspects of a relationship; are not interested in nudity or thinking about sex | Are not interested in romance; become sexually aroused by nudity and thinking about sexual acts |
| Only have loving or sexual feelings for men | Only have loving or sexual feelings for women |

The list could go on and on. You may think that some of the characteristics are exaggerated, but such attitudes have been very commonly held by a great many people. In some ways, it was probably easier to become a man or woman a few years back because the rules for your behavior were so specifically spelled out! However, I am very glad that you will have the chance to think through very carefully what kind of woman or man you want to be and then have a better opportunity to make the decisions and take the directions which will get you there.

### Jason, Lisa, Scott, and Julie

What is expected of men and women today? What does it mean to be "masculine" or "feminine" now? I recently had the privilege of discussing these questions with four high school students, and I am now bringing portions of that discussion to you. Jason and Lisa are high school seniors and seventeen years old. Scott and Julie are juniors, aged seventeen and sixteen respectively. I think that what they have to say is quite representative of current values on masculinity and femininity:

Lisa:    Sometimes, I don't know how to act anymore. I think it used to be easier when girls were supposed to act certain ways and boys were too.

Julie:   But so much of that was phony, Lisa. What about girls like me? I don't particularly care for dresses, and I'm good at playing tennis. Before, I would have been a real outcast unless I dressed up in frilly clothes and let boys win when I played tennis with them. You know, girls were supposed to be dainty and not very competitive.

Jason: That probably wasn't true for all boys. If a guy feels all right about himself, then it shouldn't matter if he gets beat by a girl in tennis or not.

Julie: Well, I was exaggerating. But the point is, now we are being encouraged to be whatever kind of girl—or person—we are.

Scott: But I kind of like girls who are a little shy, and I like feeling strong and protective toward them. If I ever do get married, I sure don't want to do much of the cooking and cleaning either.

Julie: So you would be willing to let your wife do all the dirty work!

Lisa: It isn't dirty work if you like it. I like to feel protected by a boy, and I like to cook. I'm not very competitive when it comes to sports. Lately, I've been feeling like there's something wrong with being this way.

Julie: Do you think you would always be happy doing things *for* a guy and having him always be the winner in everything?

Gary: I'm not certain that was quite what Lisa was saying, Julie.

Lisa: No, it wasn't. I enjoy cooking, and I'm good at it. That's something I can share with a husband and other people, and feel good about myself for. He can be good at different things and feel good about himself too.

Gary: I guess that is the real key to a good relationship between two people. the both of you being able to feel good about yourselves and each other.

Jason: I don't think that I could feel very good about a girl who was only interested in cooking, sewing, and other traditional "girl things." I want to be with someone who is involved in life—in the world. That way, we both have lives of our own and interesting things to talk about with one another.

Scott:   Then isn't that the kind of girl you should look for? But other guys may want to look for other types of girls.

Julie:   Getting back to what you were saying a minute ago, Scott. Did you mean that you wouldn't help out around the house?

Scott:   Not necessarily. That would depend on a lot of things. If I was the only one working at a job, then probably my wife should take care of the household stuff. If she worked too, then we could either hire someone to help out around the house, or we would share the work. Only I don't like to cook or clean.

Gary:    Again, maybe the important thing would be to have the kind of communication that would permit you to work it out together so you both are reasonably satisfied.

Julie:   But there have to be compromises, and we sometimes may have to do some types of work we don't like.

Gary:    True. We're getting a bit away from talking about femininity and masculinity, though. Things are certainly changing with regard to how girls and women are "supposed" to be. How about the ways boys and men are "supposed" to be.

Jason:   Same thing. I don't think boys have to put on the big act anymore. You know—tough, silent, unemotional, always in control. I cry sometimes and I don't have to feel ashamed that crying is "unmanly." I like art and some classical music, and I don't like football. But now, it's okay for me to be that way. I know I'm still a boy, and that's the main thing.

Julie:   There are still some things which are considered feminine. Things like sewing and ballet, for example. That's stupid, because it might save men a lot of money and trouble if they could sew, and ballet dancers have to be very strong, athletic, and competitive.

Scott:   A lot of it seems to be in the way you're brought up.

Gary:    Yes, how are we taught to be masculine or feminine from the time we are very young?

Lisa:    Girls are given dolls and toy stoves to play with, and boys are given baseball gloves and toy guns.

Jason: Boys aren't allowed to cry as much as girls, and they are encouraged to be braver about everything.

Julie: Those are the old ways. If I have children, I don't see any reason to raise the boys any differently from the girls. I'll let them have whatever interests they seem to develop. I just want them to be good people who will care about other people—not robots who are playing some game of being boys and girls.

Gary: You seem to be saying that there really aren't many inborn differences between boys and girls except for the differences in their bodies. As a matter of fact, many studies are coming to light which seem to support that idea on many counts.

Lisa: But we have still learned many of the more traditional boy and girl roles.

Gary: And those roles may be very much a part of the persons we are. There is nothing wrong with roles as long as they are a real part of you—not just some act to please someone else—and as long as they feel right and comfortable for your life.

Scott: How do you know if something is really part of you now or whether it is just something you do to fit in? Sometimes when I'm doing something the way a guy is expected to do . . .

Gary: For example?

Scott: . . . like playing hockey. Well, I sometimes feel right in the middle of a game as if I don't even want to be doing it. It's as if the only reason I'm involved is to show that I am a guy.

Jason: I think what it really means to be a man is to know yourself and what you want for your life, then to carry through with it. And it doesn't matter if you play hockey or sew or tiptoe through the tulips with pink satin slippers!

Julie: That goes for being a woman, too. Women can like hockey, and you shouldn't have to have big breasts or go to bed with guys to prove that you're a woman.

Scott: That part also applies to guys. You don't have to have a lot of sexual experience to be a guy. Sometimes I think that we're still expected to know everything about sex so we can teach girls, but it shouldn't be that way. Everybody should learn about sex, but what you do with it is still up to you.

These young people expressed some important ideas concerning trends in today's society. Some people have preferred to ignore the larger implications of the feminist movement. They claim instead that it is an uproar by a few radical, man-hating women who have nothing better to do with their time. Actually, the "movement" is the product of women from many different backgrounds throughout North America and around the world who are asking for equal treatment as individuals. They no longer are willing to be considered inferior to men in any way. All people deserve the same opportunities for personal fulfillment and satisfaction, regardless of their sex. So the central issue is not whether men should open doors for women, whether wives should have jobs while their husbands stay home with the kids, or whether women should be interested in sports. Instead it is the freedom for each of us—both women and men—to be the full person he or she is capable of being.

Part of finding and understanding your own sexuality must be deciding what masculinity and femininity mean to you. There are many influences on your life which must be considered: parents, peers, religious teachings, and your community. But most importantly, you must stay in touch with your own feelings about your own womanhood or manhood. At the end of this chapter, you will find some questions and activities which may help you sort through these areas of your life.

### Sexual Behavior and Responsibility

Another aspect of understanding our sexuality is knowing where our sexual feelings fit into our lives and how we express them. In the last chapter, two forms of sexual behavior were discussed: masturbation and sexual intercourse between a man and woman, the latter also being known as *coitus*. There are other forms of sexual expression which will be discussed later in this book. Through the years, the various forms of behavior have been judged by many different moral codes. In other words, different societies have judged them to be right or wrong.

We live in times where there are great differences in opinion concerning the rightness or wrongness of sexual activities. There are those who believe that any form of sexual behavior is right as long as it feels good, those who believe that the only permissible or right form of sex is intercourse after marriage, and those who fall somewhere in between those two extremes. Again, you will have to think carefully about where you fit in that spectrum of beliefs, now and in the future. This book will inform you about the facts concerning human sexuality and give you opportunities to think through your values. But the wondering and confusion about what you want for your life still has to be yours.

Nevertheless, we have to give these questions our careful attention before we are faced with sexual decisions. To be a responsible person, we have to take time to weigh our needs and desires with the teachings of those who are important in our lives. Then we can at least begin to make decisions which are based on thought and planning. Yet, as always, our decisions are our own.

### Human Sexual Response

To understand your sexuality more fully, it is essential to know how your body responds when it is aroused by sexual feelings. Until quite recently, there was little reliable scientific information available about sexual response. However, in 1966 Dr. William Masters and Virginia Johnson published a book titled *Human Sexual Response,* based on ten years of research into how the human body reacts during masturbation and intercourse. During their study, Masters and Johnson and their assistants observed nearly 700 men and women having sexual intercourse and masturbating. These individuals volunteered to participate in the study, and sensitive medical devices were used to measure and record the many changes which occurred in their bodies. Masters and Johnson found that the bodies of both males and females go through a predictable cycle of sexual response, summarized below.

For easier understanding of sexual response, it is helpful to divide the cycle into four distinct stages: Excitement, Plateau, Orgasm (or climax), and Resolution. It should be understood, however, that there are no distinct divisions between these stages. Figure 3.1 graphically shows the four stages.

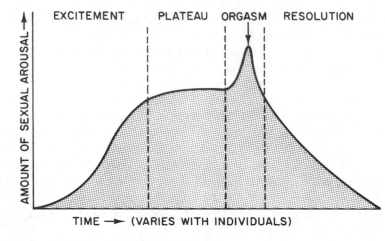

EXCITEMENT        PLATEAU    ORGASM    RESOLUTION

AMOUNT OF SEXUAL AROUSAL →

TIME → (VARIES WITH INDIVIDUALS)

**Figure 3.1**    The Sexual Response Cycle.

Now we shall consider what happens during each stage:

1. *Excitement.*    In slang, this phase is often referred to as getting "turned on." There is an increase in muscular tension throughout the body, and the nipples of both males and females may become harder and erect. Many women and men experience a "blushing" of the skin on the chest, abdomen, and neck, known as the "sex flush." The heart begins to beat faster and blood pressure goes up somewhat.

In males, the most obvious sign of sexual excitement is erection of the penis (see page 14). In females, the inner walls of the vagina undergo a "sweating" reaction and become somewhat wet, while the width and length of the vagina increase by about 25%. The clitoris of the female also becomes erect. All of these reactions are the result of an increased flow of blood into the pelvic area.

2. *Plateau.*    During this stage, the changes begun during excitement become more intense. Muscular tension in the body increases, along with heart rate and blood pressure. The rate

of breathing has usually increased by this stage too. The reddening of the sex flush may appear now if it has not before.

In males, the testes are pulled up closer to the body in the scrotum, and the head of the penis becomes more swollen with blood than before. A few drops of the clear secretion from Cowper's glands may appear at the tip of the penis. In females, the clitoris pulls back under the folds of skin that cover its shaft, and the amount of lubrication in the vagina may increase. Both the scrotum and vulval lips swell somewhat with the increased blood flow into their tissues.

3. *Orgasm* or *Climax.* This is one of the most difficult parts of human sexual response to describe. Although orgasm lasts only a few seconds, it is one of the most intensely pleasurable experiences in human sensation. During orgasm, the muscular tension which has built up during excitement and plateau is released.

At the time of orgasm, the body has reached a peak of tension. In the male, muscles at the base of the penis in the ejaculatory duct contract to push semen out of the penis—ejaculation. The first three or four contractions are the strongest and occur slightly less than a second apart. Then the contractions become less intense and farther apart. Females also experience such contractions in the vagina, and may sometimes even emit a small amount of fluid that has collected there. While these pleasurable contractions are occurring, the body muscles of both males and females may be involuntarily contracting—often quite strongly. The entire pelvic area may undergo thrusting movements. The individual may gasp or cry out. A pleasant "tickling" sensation is usually felt throughout the body. People report that they have different types of orgasms at different times, some being more powerful and pleasurable than others. Some people also enjoy sexual activity without reaching orgasm at all.

4. *Resolution.* Immediately following orgasm, the body begins to return to its state before sexual excitement began. The muscles become very relaxed within about five minutes, while heart rate, blood pressure, and breathing all return to their typical rates. Gradually, the sex flush disappears and the nipples lose their erection.

In males, the penis loses about half of its erect size within a short period of time. Then, more gradually, the penis returns to its non-excited size and limpness. The testes relax and move slightly down from the body again. Males also go through a period known as the *refractory period*, during which they cannot reach orgasm again. This period may be very brief (a few minutes) or last longer (hours), depending on the male's age, degree of sexual stimulation, and individual sexual needs.

In females, resolution includes the return of the clitoris to its regular position almost immediately and the return of the vagina to its unstimulated size within ten or fifteen minutes. However, unlike males, females do not have a refractory period, and some may reach orgasm more than once during a single sexual experience.

### Individual Differences in Sexual Response

Whenever an individual is sexually aroused and is stimulated to reach orgasm, he or she goes through the stages described above. The stages occur regardless of the means of sexual stimulation: masturbation, intercourse, or other shared physical contact. There may be some variations in the details of the stages, especially in females. The most pronounced differences, however, are in the amount of time which various individuals take for the sexual response cycle. It is possible for some individuals to move through the entire cycle—from excitement to resolution—in a very few minutes, while others may spend an hour or more in the cycle. How long the cycle takes depends on many circumstances, including what the person has learned regarding his or her own sexual pleasure.

It should also be mentioned that other researchers have preferred to use a two-phase model rather than the four-phase one that Masters and Johnson designed. The two-phase approach simply describes the build up of blood in the pelvic organs and the increase in muscular tension, followed by reversal of blood congestion and relaxation of the tension after orgasm.

### Masturbation

You will recall that masturbation refers to self-stimulation of the sex organs to produce sexual arousal and, usually, orgasm.

Many young people first get in touch with their sexual feelings through masturbation. Studies have shown that nearly all boys and the majority of girls masturbate quite regularly. A boy most often masturbates by grasping his penis with his hand and stroking it or by rubbing his penis against some object. A girl usually masturbates by stroking her clitoris or the surrounding area or by massaging the entire area of the vulva. Many boys, girls, men, and women experiment with a great variety of ways to masturbate. Most people fantasize (daydream) about things which they find sexually exciting while they masturbate.

Unfortunately, masturbation is not often talked about and consequently many misunderstandings have developed about it. For many years, some adults—thinking masturbation to be immoral—told youngsters wild stories about the frightening consequences of masturbation. These myths included claims that masturbation would cause pimples, insanity, mental retardation, and physical weakness! Other myths, perhaps less frightening but just as false, persist today. These include the ideas that masturbation will weaken you so you will not be as successful in athletic endeavors and that "too much" masturbation will cause a boy to run out of sperm so he will not be able to produce children. All are totally untrue. Another myth is that only youngsters masturbate, and when they establish mature relationships, masturbation ceases. The fact is, most adults continue masturbating occasionally throughout their lives, and often into old age.

In years past, people were so convinced that masturbation was bad and dangerous, parents would take extreme measures to prevent their children from masturbating. Devices were designed to prevent youngsters from touching their sex organs—including metal mitts to put on their hands at bedtime and various sorts of belts (chastity belts) which were placed over their sex organs.

Fortunately, times have changed. Most physicians and other professionals agree that masturbation is a normal and effective outlet for sexual tension. There is also no such thing as "too much" masturbation. Some people masturbate only a few times per year, while others masturbate several times a day. Some people choose not to masturbate at all. Different individuals have different sexual needs. Apparently there is no harm to mind or body, regardless of the frequency with which masturbation is practiced. Contrary to popular opinion, there are also no laws which prohibit masturbation in private.

Some of the negative attitudes toward masturbation still exist, however. As a result, some individuals are still left with some guilt or anxiety each time they masturbate. Of course, over a period of time, such feelings may build up to some fairly negative attitudes about oneself. If you have been troubled by such feelings, perhaps it would help to talk them out with someone you can trust. See "Finding a Counselor," pages 88-91.

Again, it will be up to you to decide how masturbation is to fit—or not fit—into your life. It is okay not to masturbate as well. Some religious teachings hold that masturbation is immoral and should not be practiced. If these beliefs are a part of your background, you may want to give them appropriate consideration.

Many professionals today believe that masturbation has benefits. They feel that the practice helps young people to understand and become better acquainted with their sexual feelings. Additionally, it is felt that masturbation may serve as a good substitute for sex with another person before the young man or woman is emotionally ready for that step in a relationship. If boys use masturbation to learn how to prolong the amount of time it takes to reach orgasm—instead of hurrying to finish—they may be learning how to be better sexual partners for future relationships. Girls may learn how to reach orgasm through masturbation, and that ability may be transferred to satisfying sexual contacts later.

### Decision-making and Your Sexuality

Several times already in this book, it has been stated that you will have to figure out what you want for your life—now and in the future. In other words, *you* are the one who is going to have to make the decisions of what you want to do with your sexuality. There will be plenty of people who will try to persuade you one way or another, but the final decision always rests with you. That is a fact of life which can even be scary at times because it also means that we have to take responsibility for the consequences of our decisions. There is a great variety of sexual things that people can do and feel. The next chapter begins to explore the varieties of sexual inclinations and behaviors that human beings may have. We will also attempt to explore the possible consequences of sexual behavior as we go along, both positive and negative. I hope you will consider this information carefully as you make the sexual decisions for your life.

### Who Are You as a Sexual Person?
The following exercises can help you clarify and understand your own sexuality if you do them with careful thought. Most of them could also be used with a friend or in a group of people who would like to talk over these issues together.

1. *Masculine — Feminine*
   a. Examine the following list of qualities and decide which you want for yourself as a man or woman: (Add words of your own if you wish).

| | | |
|---|---|---|
| honest | physically strong | responsible |
| brave | dominating | emotional |
| athletic | delicate | persuasive |
| loving | intelligent | protective |
| competitive | successful | shy |
| gentle | submissive | reliable |
| sensitive | manipulative | flighty |
| aggressive | thoughtful | sincere |
| considerate | confident | sexy |

   b. Now, read through the list of qualities again and pick out those which have been traditionally considered masculine and those traditionally considered feminine. Make two separate lists on a sheet of paper. Some words may appear on both lists or neither. Again, include any words you have added to the list.
   c. Finally, note where the qualities you picked for yourself in (a) fall in your two lists. Think about them. This should help to show how your goals for your own masculinity or femininity relate to traditional ideas about men and women, as you view them.

2. *You and Your Parents*
   Spend some time thinking about your parents' ideas of what is masculine and feminine: what they consider appropriate for women and men. How are your ideas the same and how do they differ? Perhaps you will want to talk over these thoughts with your parents.

3. *How do you react?*
   Read each of the following statements and think about them. How do you react to them? Do you agree or disagree, and how strongly? Perhaps you could discuss them in a classroom or other situation:
   a. A recent newspaper story reported that a Superintendent of Schools in a Minnesota community directed his teachers and counselors "to teach such values as preservation of the family unit with the feminine role of wife, mother and homemaker and masculine role of guide, protector and provider."
   b. A group of boys in a gym class discovered another boy masturbating in a locker room bathroom. He was obviously embarrassed, but the boys who discovered him continued to joke about the incident for weeks after.

4. *Making Decisions*
   a. You may already have made some decisions about sex for your life. For example, you may have decided whether or not you want to masturbate or engage in sexual activity with someone. Are you still satisfied with your decision(s)? What things did you consider in making your decision? Do you ever consider re-thinking the decision and changing your mind? Why? Would your parents be happy with your decision?
   b. Next time you are facing any kind of decision, take some time to try a *fantasy*. Find a quiet place where you can relax and close your eyes. Then, try to picture two individuals in your mind, arguing the various points on all sides of the question. You may be surprised at the characters your imagination produces—they may not even be people. In any case, pay careful attention to what you visualize in your "mind's eye." What do the fantasy char-

acters look like; how big is each; which argues the loudest and most convincingly? Such a fantasy may tell you a great deal about how you make decisions. Give it a try!

## For Further Reading

Carlson, D. *Loving Sex for Both Sexes.* New York: Franklin Watts, 1979.

CHOICE. *Changes: You and Your Body* (Booklet written with teenagers). Philadelphia, PA: CHOICE (1501 Cherry Street), 1978.

Eagan, Andrea B. *Why Am I So Miserable If These Are the Best Years of My Life?* New York: Avon Books, 1979.

Hunt, Morton. *What is a Man? What is a Woman?* New York: Farrar, Straus, and Giroux, 1979.

Madaras, Lynda and Madaras, Area. *What's Happening to My Body? A Growing Up Guide for Mothers and Daughters.* New York: Newmarket Press, 1983.

Madaras, Lynda and Saavedra, Dane. *The What's Happening to My Body? Book for Boys.* New York: Newmarket Press, 1984.

Morrison, Eleanor, *et al. Growing Up Sexual.* New York: D. Van Nostrand, 1980.

# 4   Different Strokes for Different Folks

You have noticed how the kinds of food you like and dislike are different from some of those other people like and dislike. Some people relish foods such as mushrooms, caviar, wines, and spinach; others find them unpleasant to the taste. Some people feel very hungry most of the time, while others need to eat very little. It is much the same with the sexual appetites of human beings. What is a sexual turn-on for one individual may be a real turn-off for another. While some of us are interested in sex most of the time, others seldom feel such interest.

In this chapter, we shall explore the different sorts of sexual preferences people have. It may be too early for you to know fully what kinds of things you will find sexually interesting, but wherever you stand now, it is important to understand the varieties of sexual behavior which human beings experience.

### What is "Normal"?

It seems that we spend a lot of our time wondering whether or not we are "normal." Are we too tall? too short? too thin? too fat? Boys wonder if their penises are normal; girls wonder if their breasts are normal. We wonder about our sexual thoughts and feelings too.

Professionals who work with people have difficulty defining what is normal and what is not. One way to do it is by gathering statistics: if a large number of people fit a particular pattern, then it is "normal." But there are some flaws in that approach. Assume that a study is done which shows that 98% of fifteen-year-olds in the U.S. like pizza. Would that mean that the "abnormal" few who do not like pizza are sick? When it comes to sexual behavior in our society, there are still some fairly strong ideas about what patterns may be considered "normal" and "healthy." However, the facts are that millions of people simply do not fit these patterns and yet continue to live happy, productive lives. We must begin to realize fully that each of us has his or her own legitimate set of sexual attitudes and feelings.

Most professionals in the field of human sexuality today seem to agree on one thing: that an individual's sexual orientations and behaviors need not be considered unhealthy unless they are causing physical or emotional harm to that individual or to others. At various times in our lives, most of us experience some concern or worry about our sexuality. That does not mean that our sexual feelings or attitudes have made us "sick." It simply means that it might be a good idea to talk over our concerns with a friend or counselor (see pages 88-91).

A small percentage of people do adopt types of sexual behavior that are dangerous or hurtful to others. These are discussed in more detail in Chapter Seven of this book. Such individuals may require special professional help.

### Learning Our Sexual Preferences

We do not yet fully understand how our individual sexual preferences develop. There may even be some influences on our sexual feelings before we are born. For the most part, however, it seems that our sexual interests and preferences are learned over a long period of time, especially during childhood. During our first few years of life, many parts of our sexual nature are well-established in our personalities. Once established, many of those parts stick with us for a lifetime, others change.

It is important to emphasize, however, that we may also exert control over our sexual impulses. Sometimes in films and literature, people are portrayed as being at the mercy of their sexual feelings, being led into wild sexual encounters by uncontrollable instincts. That view is inaccurate. Human beings are capable of making responsible decisions about what they want to do sexually. Our sexual feelings are very strong and influential in our lives, but well within whatever controls we want to place on them. The point is, then, that we are all capable of finding happiness and satisfaction in our sexuality, and it may take some work to accomplish that.

Another important thing to remember is the changing nature of our sexuality. Over the years, our preferences for certain foods may change. Similarly—although perhaps not as simply—our values and preferences for certain sexual things may change too, depending on our circumstances, relationships with others, and our own changing needs. This does not mean that if there is something about our sexuality we do not like, that it will just pass away in time or that we can force it to change. If you are dissatisfied with parts of your sexuality, it may be the right time to think and talk about them and to understand them more fully. In time, you might even become more accepting of the sexual person you are.

### Sex and Aging

Young people often have difficulty realizing that adults—even older adults—have sexual needs. We do not lose our ability to feel sexually or to enjoy those feelings at any particular age. Our sexual preferences may change, our degree of interest in sex may change, but we are sexual people all of our lives. We may experience sexual joys and sexual worries at any age.

As people get older, their degree of interest in sex may decrease gradually and physical illness may hinder their enjoyment of sex. However, most people retain their potential to enjoy

sexual feelings, including touching and caressing, even into their 70s, 80s, or beyond. Getting acquainted with the changes of our sexuality is a lifetime proposition.

### Sexual Thoughts, Fantasies, and Pictures

At one point or another in their lives, most people worry that they are thinking about sex too much. They may experience fantasies (daydreams) or dreams during sleep about sex, some of which may include pretty wild activities. The important thing to keep in mind is that most people think and fantasize about sex. That is nothing to worry about or apologize for. Our fantasies—even our wildest ones—cannot hurt anyone. It is our actions for which we must be responsible and about which decisions must be made. At times, our fantasies and thoughts may give us clues about what we find sexually interesting, but they are just portions of our imagination—nothing to be feared.

Some individuals enjoy looking at pictures of people who are nude or engaged in sexual acts. Such materials are available in magazines, movie films, video tapes, slides, and other forms and are often referred to as *pornography*. That term means that the material is of a sexual nature which may be sexually arousing for some people. Others find such materials offensive and obscene and feel that they should not be made available to anyone.

There have been many laws passed and court decisions made about pornography, but as things now stand, many sexually oriented pictures and gadgets are available to those who want to pay for them.

In 1968, a Presidential Commission was established to study obscenity and pornography. The majority of Commission members reported that viewing pictures of a sexual nature had not been proven to have any harmful effects on people, regardless of their age. There was no evidence that viewing pornography leads to sex crimes. More recently, new controversies have developed, and citizen groups are still calling for bans on sexually explicit materials. Some people feel that pornography offers a distorted view of sexual relations because of its emphasis on the purely physical aspects of sex. Others feel that most pornography reflects a rather negative view of women, and is demeaning to them.

It should be kept in mind that pornography does not adequately portray what really goes on between most people sexually, nor does it emphasize the importance of a healthy, communicative relationship as a basis for sexual sharing. If such material is the only outlet for sexual feelings, to the exclusion of meaningful relationships with other people, then the individual may want to examine his or her needs more closely to determine if the pictures have become a kind of escape.

### Extreme Curiosity

From the time we are very young, most of us are interested in what the nude bodies of others look like. We are curious to see their sex organs, not only those of the opposite sex, but others of our own. That curiosity is natural and normal. It is especially predictable in a culture which does not encourage nudity. For some people, however, this natural curiosity is carried to extremes which offend others. They invade the privacy of others by peeking through windows, hoping to catch a glimpse of someone in the nude. This may be done by groups of young people for fun or by an individual who feels a desperate need to do so. If a person is caught peering in someone's window, they could be subject to arrest and prosecution, so it is a practice that carries with it some dangers. As much as many of us enjoy looking at other's bodies, it would be sensible to choose a method of doing so which is not frightening or embarrassing to others and not in violation of their right to privacy.

### Same Sex Behavior

One of the "rules" which is accepted by our society is that people should be sexually interested only in those of the opposite sex. Again, the facts are different from what the "rule" suggests should be true. There are many who experience sexual interest in someone of their same sex. That interest may be expressed as simple curiosity about the other person's body or through strong feelings of love and attachment that involve sexual desires or actual sexual experience.

Younger boys and girls often play games with one another which lead to undressing and touching each other's sex organs. The old stand-by game of "doctor" is among the most common. Such games apparently are generally harmless and represent ways to learn about the body. Sometimes as a part of these games, children of the same sex examine and touch one another.

As children grow older and begin to experience sexual feelings more strongly, there may be some experimentation with sex. That experimentation may be between youngsters of opposite sexes or of the same sex. It is very common for two boys or two girls to examine each others' bodies, including the sex organs, and to become sexually aroused by doing so. This often leads to masturbating together or other forms of sexual experimentation. For many youth, this is a common occurrence in their development. Such experimentation sometimes occurs in groups of youngsters. Many boys and girls develop a strong interest in and attachment to an adult of either sex. This is a very common aspect of development, and such "crushes" generally fade with time.

Some individuals continue to have sexual interest in others of their own sex into adulthood. Many men and women occasionally experience thoughts or fantasies about having sexual contact with others of the same sex. A major study of sexual behavior tells us that about 37% of men and 28% of women carry through on these desires at some point in their adult lives and have a same-sex experience to the point of orgasm. Some individuals find that they are generally more aroused sexually by members of their own sex and prefer them as sexual partners over those of the opposite sex. Such individuals are called *homosexuals*; female homosexuals are sometimes referred to as *lesbians*.

### Homosexuality

Homosexuality is poorly understood in today's society. Homosexuals are often unjustly considered to be sick and dangerous, being labeled with such slang terms as "queer," "faggot," or "dyke." As a result of these negative attitudes, many men and women who have homosexual preferences are made to feel guilty and afraid. Because they may be frightened of having others discover their "secret," some homosexuals do not allow themselves to develop close relationships.

In recent years, however, attitudes toward homosexuality have been changing. This has been partly the result of the educational efforts of groups of homosexuals. Since another popular term for homosexual is "gay," such groups are often called Gay Liberation groups or Gay Alliances. The men and women in these groups have pointed out how unfair laws and social prejudices have caused serious discrimination against homosexuals. Most states no longer have such laws.

Another reason for the changing attitudes is the availability of more accurate information about homosexual behavior. Most psychologists and counselors no longer consider homosexuality to be a sickness that must be changed. Instead, it is recognized to be a valid life-style which seems suitable for those who prefer to love and have sexual relationships with others of their own sex.

Like most other aspects of human sexuality, neither homosexual nor heterosexual (opposite sex) behavior is an all-or-nothing thing. Studies done prior to the changed attitudes about homosexuality showed that 4-6% of men and 2-4% of women remained exclusively homosexual throughout their lives, while 63% of men and 72% of women remained exclusively heterosexual. So it is clear that many people have established both homosexual and heterosexual relationships at various times in their lives. Individuals who continue to maintain both kinds of sexual relationships are usually called *bisexuals*.

Many homosexuals who discover their preferences later in life see their heterosexual experience (often quite extensive) as having been largely a matter of convenience—an effort to conform to the prevailing rules and attitudes of the society they lived in. Sometimes, homosexual behavior also seems to be a matter of convenience, as in prisons, where men and women may develop temporary homosexual relationships.

Many myths still exist about homosexuality. One of those myths is that homosexuals may be identified by their appearance or mannerisms. In fact, boys who have high-pitched voices, walk with a "girlish" gait, and do not enjoy sports are not necessarily homosexual. Girls who have deeper voices, enjoy sports and outdoor activities, and dress in "boyish" clothes are not necessarily homosexual. Likewise, very strong, "manly" males and dainty, "feminine" females are not necessarily heterosexual. There is apparently no particular relationship between a person's appearance and his or her sexual orientation.

Another myth is that homosexuals "hate" members of the opposite sex. In fact, most homosexuals develop friendships—even loving relationships—with those of the opposite sex. Neither are homosexuals more prone to the seduction of children and teenagers than are heterosexual individuals. Some youngsters—particulary boys—have been frightened by being asked by an adult to participate in some homosexual act. Although this may be upsetting, the older person will seldom push the issue if told, "no, it's just not for me." Studies show that a far greater proportion of sexual approaches to children are made by heterosexuals. More about that in Chapter Seven.

Other false information leads to the belief that all male dancers, hairdressers, and interior decorators are homosexuals, and that all female truck drivers and armed service officers are lesbians. Usually these individuals are simply heterosexuals who have broken through the traditional occupational stereotypes of men and women.

### Being a Homosexual
The reasons why a person grows up with strong homosexual feelings are not understood. Many theories have been advanced

by professionals, but none has been fully accepted. One current idea is that most human beings have the potential for both heterosexual and homosexual attraction, and that most of us learn to be heterosexual because our culture finds that pattern more acceptable. Nevertheless, research studies continue to confirm that about 10% of the adult population is predominantly homosexual in their sexual orientation. Whatever the causes, homosexuality and heterosexuality probably become estabished in the personality during childhood.

An individual may become aware of his or her homosexual leanings quite early in life or later. Some homosexuals are aware of their intense feelings a long time before they fully admit the feelings to themselves or others. When a person is concerned or confused about homosexual feelings, it is often helpful to talk with an understanding counselor. It should be realized that individuals who have mostly homosexual feelings cannot usually be led toward having only heterosexual inclinations. However, good counseling can help homosexuals and bisexuals to understand and accept their sexuality more completely, and also to choose the kinds of sexual life-styles that suit them best. (See "Finding a Counselor" in Chapter Six.)

When homosexuals—young or old—are facing and sorting through their sexuality, many questions must be carefully considered. For example, they must decide whom they wish to tell about their sexual orientation. More often than not, family and friends are quite accepting of an individual's homosexuality when they are helped to understand it. Gay organizations often provide group meetings for parents and other family members to help with the accepting process. Sometimes, however, homosexuals experience rejection and anger from those around them. There are still many forms of discrimination against homosexuals, so caution about who is told may be advisable, especially if practical considerations such as employment might be in jeopardy.

Many homosexuals have difficulty in finding other homosexuals, especially in rural areas. For this reason, they sometimes must cope with loneliness. (Heterosexuals often find it difficult to find suitable partners also, and experience the same kind of loneliness.) In cities, special counseling centers and social groups for homosexuals are often available which may aid in these concerns (see page 187).

It should be understood that most homosexuals, like most heterosexuals, are not interested solely in sex with their partners. They search for warm, friendly companionship and are often interested in more lasting loving relationships. Some homosexual couples live together for many years, sharing love, sex, household duties, and finances, much as some heterosexual couples do. Marriage of homosexuals has not yet achieved much legal recognition, and is discussed in more detail in Chapter Nine.

### Cross-Dressing

Some people enjoy dressing in clothes of the opposite sex. This may be done as a gag, such as for a Halloween costume, or may have more sexual implications. Some homosexuals cross-dress occasionally for fun; they are then said to be "in drag."

There are some people who get sexual satisfaction from dressing in clothes usually worn by members of the opposite sex. These people are called *transvestites,* and only a small proportion of them are homosexuals. Although transvestism is harmless to others, there are laws which permit the arrest and prosecution of transvestites in some cities and states.

### Transsexualism

Transsexualism should not be confused with homosexuality. The transsexual is a person who feels that he or she has the personality of the opposite sex. Transsexuals often feel from the time they are very young as if they are trapped in the wrong body, and this may lead to frustration and depression. With the true transsexual, counseling or psychotherapy aimed at helping the individual to accept the body he or she was born with is not generally effective. It is sometimes advisable for transsexuals to undergo treatment at medical centers where their bodies may gradually be changed by hormonal and surgical treatment to resemble a body of the opposite sex. Several thousand people in the United States have undergone surgery to alter their bodies and sex organs in this way.

### Prostitution

Prostitution refers to participation in sexual acts for money. It has existed for thousands of years and is sometimes jokingly called the "world's oldest profession." Most prostitutes are women, paid to have sex with men, although some male prostitutes are also available for women. There are homosexual prostitutes too. There are many reasons why people have sexual contact with prostitutes. Regardless of the reason, it is obviously a casual form of sex, with little emotional involvement between the partners. It is primarily a physical experience rather than a total sexual encounter involving feelings and the whole personality.

Studies over the past thirty years have shown that the percentage of young men who have contact with prostitutes has dropped sharply, probably the result of changing sex-related values in our culture.

Of course, there is always the danger of contracting a sexually transmitted disease (STD) (see Chapter Seven) from a prostitute. One of the arguments in favor of legalized prostitution is that legalization would permit the government to establish regulations requiring constant STD checks on prostitutes.

In cities, houses of prostitution are usually available, also called "brothels" or "houses of ill-repute." Since prostitutes are also termed whores, such houses are sometimes called "whorehouses." A person who arranges customers for prostitutes is called a pimp.

### Other Sexual Preferences

When it comes to sexual "turn-ons"—things that are sexually arousing and interesting—human beings are remarkable for their diversity. Many people associate various odors or objects with sexual excitement, such as perfumes, or soft blankets, or leather objects. There is no particular harm in finding such things sexually arousing as long as they do not detract from the sexual sharing which may be a part of close loving relationships.

Although there may be some roughness and strenuous physical activity in many sexual encounters, some people have come to associate discomfort, some degree of pain, or humiliation with sexual arousal. This sexual orientation is termed *sadomasochism,* or *S and M.* The sadist has traditionally been thought of as the individual who inflicts the pain or humiliation, while the masochist is the one who is submissive. It is quite common, however, for S and M partners to play either role at various times, and so we refer to such individuals as sado-masochists. Sado-masochistic partners frequently act out sex-related scenes with one another, involving imaginary situations in which one takes the dominant, overbearing role while the other acts meek and submissive. The scenes may involve pretending to "force" one partner into having sexual acts. Another variation on the S and M theme is *bondage*, which involves tying a person during sex or binding particular parts of the body to create pressure.

Sado-masochism may be very acceptable and safe for sexual partners who know each other's needs and have established agreements for what they want from each other. Some professionals, however, have argued that S and M is unhealthy because of its connections with pain and inequality in the sexual relationship. The obvious dangers lie in possible unintentional physical injury that could occur, or in an exploitative relationship where one person forces a partner into acts in which she or he does not want to participate.

There are a number of other human sexual preferences. However, there are few reliable statistics to tell us just how common these preferences are. For example, a few research studies have indicated that a fair percentage of people probably have some sort of sexual contact with an animal during their lifetimes, particulary boys who live on farms. There are no indications that such animal contacts are harmful, except for the obvious dangers of poor hygiene, injury by the animal or to the animal, or guilt on the part of the human. Again, laws do exist prohibiting sexual contact with animals, often called bestiality or zoophilia.

Many forms of sexual behavior are not considered acceptable to many people in our society, including some of the preferences discussed in this chapter. Those forms of behavior which are generally considered to be unhealthy and harmful to others are discussed in Chapter Seven, especially pages 99-101. It should be remembered that any form of sexual behavior may have its unhealthy aspects unless it is understood, accepted, and responsibly enjoyed by the individual and is not harmful or guilt-producing to that individual or others.

**Where Are You Now? A Questionnaire**

The following questionnaire is meant for *your own use.* Do not write answers in the book for others to see. You should not be asked to share answers with anyone else—even anonymously. If you choose to talk over your answers with a trusted friend, that, of course, is up to you.

How would you answer the following questions? Think about your answers carefully. There are no "right" or "wrong" answers, no "normal" or "abnormal" answers—just *your* answers.

Yes ☐ No ☐  Have you sometimes worried that you think or fantasize too much about sex?

Yes ☐ No ☐  Do you think that your sexual fantasies are "wild"?

Yes ☐ No ☐  Do you enjoy looking at pictures of nude people or sexy scenes?

Yes ☐ No ☐  Have you ever felt sexually aroused by another person of your own sex?

Yes ☐ No ☐  Have you ever participated in sex play with a person of your own sex?

Yes ☐ No ☐  If so, did you feel upset or guilty about it?

Yes ☐ No ☐  Do you often think about having a sexual experience with someone of the opposite sex?

Yes ☐ No ☐  Have you ever participated in sex play with a person of the opposite sex?

Yes ☐ No ☐  If so, did you feel upset or guilty about it?

Yes ☐ No ☐  For the most part, are you happy with your sexuality?

At this point in your life, what things interest you most sexually? _____

At this point in your life, what sexual preferences are most difficult for you to understand and identify with?_____

_____

What would you *most* like to change about your body or sexual preferences? _____

_____

What would you *least* like to change about your body or sexual preferences? _____

**What Do You Think?**
1. Here is a list of some current issues in our society. What are your opinions on these issues?
   a. Should homosexuals be allowed to marry?
   b. Should homosexuals be allowed to adopt and raise children?
   c. Should there be laws banning the distribution, sale, or use of pornographic materials?
   d. Should prostitution be made legal?
2. Try to project yourself into the following situations and think carefully about what you would think and do. How do your imagined actions reflect your feelings and values?
   a. One afternoon you are talking alone with your best friend of your same sex. Your friend confides to you that she or he is a homosexual.
   b. You are away at college (or summer camp, or working in a city) and your roommate tells you after two weeks that you probably should be told that he or she is a homosexual.
   c. One of your teachers of your same sex has become a good friend. One afternoon while talking together casually, she/he gently puts a hand on your shoulder and leaves it there for several seconds.
   d. Go back to situations a and c and try to consider what your reactions would be if the other person was of the opposite sex.

**For Further Reading**
Fricke, Aaron. *Reflections of a Rock Lobster: A Story About Growing Up Gay.* Boston: Alyson Publications, 1981.

Garden, Nancy. *Annie on My Mind* (a fictional story of love between two adolescent girls). New York: Farrar, Straus, and Giroux, 1982.

Hanckel, Frances and Cunningham, John. *A Way of Love, A Way of Life: A Young Person's Introduction to What it Means to be Gay.* New York: Lothrop, Lee, and Shepard, 1979.

Jones, Clinton R. *Understanding Gay Relatives and Friends.* New York: Seabury Press, 1978.

Kelly, Gary F. *Sexuality: The Human Perspective.* Woodbury, NY: Barron's Educational Series, 1980.

Masters, William H., Johnson, Virginia E., and Kolodny, Robert C. *Human Sexuality.* Boston: Little, Brown, 1985.

McNaught, Brian. *A Disturbed Peace: Selected Writings of an Irish Catholic Homosexual.* Washington, DC: Dignity Inc., 1981.

Meeks, Linda B. and Heit, Philip. *Human Sexuality: Making Responsible Decisions.* New York: Saunders College Publishing, 1982.

# 5    Sharing Our Sexual Feelings

Did you jump ahead? When I read books on sex, I often jump ahead to the chapters which seem most interesting to me. That's fine. You are, of course, free to do that with this book to find the topics which are most significant for you. I would like to suggest, however, that at some point you also go back and read the earlier chapters and also that you read the chapters following this one. They might help you to sort through how the material in this chapter fits into *your* life. Okay?

Since our sexuality is a part of our total personality, we bring that sexuality with us to every contact we have with another human being. In some of those contacts, we find ourselves more in touch with our actual sexual feelings and find ourselves sexually aroused ("turned-on") by the other person. The other person may be experiencing the same kind of interest, and then some decisions may be made about how much sharing of sexual feelings you both want to have.

### Levels of Sharing
Before exploring the decision-making process, it will be important to explore the different levels of sexual sharing. We shall begin with the more superficial levels and move to the deeper

levels, involving more closeness and sense of personal intimacy. It is usually safe to assume that deeper levels of sharing bring with them more implications and responsibilities to be considered carefully and thoughtfully.

An important part of early sexual sharing with another is *talking together.* This usually continues into deeper levels of sharing as well. Often, open communication of thoughts and feelings leads to the desire for more intimacy. Yet, such communication can be scary too. It takes courage to let another person in on what we are feeling and thinking. There is much more on communication about sex in Chapter Six.

After talking together, the decision might be reached that there is no point in moving to deeper levels of sexual sharing. Often, however, two people move on to some form of *body contact.* It is usually very exciting and exhilarating to get physically closer to someone whom you care about and feel sexually attracted to. For many couples, this contact begins with kissing and hugging, sometimes referred to as "necking." Sometimes during kissing, one partner may move his or her tongue into the other's mouth, often called "French kissing." All of us have our own preferences about how we like to be kissed and where we most enjoy being touched. As two people get to know each other, talking and other signals which develop help to convey those preferences to one another.

Two people who enjoy physical closeness may eventually move toward touching many parts of each other's bodies, including the sex organs. This is usually called "petting," although that term has been used in many different ways. The more touching the two people do, the more apt they are to become intensely aroused sexually. Even with very little physical contact—or just thinking about a person he finds attractive—a boy may experience sexual excitement and erection of his penis. Girls may also experience sensations of increased tension and sexual arousal of their bodies when they are physically close to someone they find attractive or are thinking about that person.

It should be kept in mind that some people may not want certain parts of their body touched, and they certainly have the right to avoid such contact. As sexual sharing deepens, it is up to both partners to keep in touch with messages from one another which indicate pleasure or displeasure. The term "heavy petting" generally refers to deliberately stimulating the other person's sex organs. This is done not only with the hands, but sometimes with the mouth. It may also refer to touching a girl's breasts. Sometimes, the touching is done through the clothing. Other times, one partner may reach inside the other's clothing or both may decide to remove their clothing. Of course, being in the nude with another person may be somewhat awkward and uncomfortable at first, but it may also be intensely pleasurable and highly sexually exciting. This represents a very deep level of sexual sharing which may carry with it strong emotions and the need for responsible decision-making.

An even deeper level of sharing comes with sexual activity in which one or both of the partners may reach orgasm. Most everyone feels that such activity is an important step in the process of sexual sharing. Yet many couples decide to postpone it for a variety of reasons, and they confine their pleasurable sharing to petting without orgasm or lighter levels of sharing. It should be remembered, however, that sexual feelings are powerful, and once we become sexually aroused, it may be much more difficult to spend much time thinking through decisions. For that reason, it is probably wise to clarify our values and our ideas about responsibility before we place ourselves in a situation which produces intense sexual excitement.

Perhaps the level of sexual sharing that is deepest of all is the one that involves loving feelings for the other person. This leads to the gentle, warm sharing of the deepest parts of ourselves. That kind of sharing may be a part of sexual activity and the quiet being together following orgasm, but not necessarily. It may also be a part of any other level of sexual sharing, regardless of how much body contact is involved. While I was writing this chapter, a friend said to me, "Let's not give young people the idea that sex is just intercourse. My wife and I love to give each other massages, and that is a really great sexual experience!" I truly hope that this whole book will help to convey that very message: sex *is* far more than intercourse or any other form of sexual activity leading to orgasm.

### Foundations of Sexual Activity

It is often difficult to find much information about what actually happens in sex, and few people readily discuss their own sexual experiences. Consequently, many young people find that sex is a rather mysterious thing. Even when it is described in books or portrayed on film, the facts may be considerably distorted. The media often show sexual activity as simple and always supremely pleasurable. In actuality, sexual activity that yields the maximum pleasure to both partners may take a considerable amount of learning, communication, and time, and may have nothing to do with the capacity of the individuals to "perform" sexually. Instead, it may depend more on the quality of the personal relationship between the people involved.

Because of the distorted view of sex which many people develop, or for other reasons, their first sexual experiences may be quite disappointing. Or, first experiences might be quite wonderful and exciting, and later experiences may be disappointing because they lack the same quality of discovery. Both kinds of disappointment may lead to discouragement and real sexual problems. So it makes sense to learn as much about the various forms of sexual activity as possible before deciding whether or not to engage in them.

Perhaps one of the most important foundations for enjoyable and meaningful sex is that *both partners really want it to happen.* They really want it to happen not because they are rushed into it, but because they have thought through their decisions carefully and shared their thoughts, feelings, and values with one another. In other words, neither partner is being persuaded into any sexual activity by reasons such as fear of "losing" the other person, wanting to prove that one is now "grown up," doing it because one's friends are, or one's selfish manipulations to "get it" from the other.

Another necessary foundation for meaningful sex is an atmosphere of relaxation, externally and internally. The external setting must be one which enables both partners to feel happy, comfortable, and good about themselves. A physically uncomfortable place, such as a cramped car seat, or an atmosphere which necessitates hurrying, such as the fear of getting caught, will probably not produce a fully pleasurable experience. Likewise, both partners should be as free from internal worries and conflicts as possible. If either person feels frightened, guilty, or as if he or she is doing something "wrong," then perhaps more time should be given to the decision of whether or not to have intercourse. It is also important to note that body hygiene is necessary for many people to enjoy sex (fresh breath, no perspiration odor, clean sex organs).

Part of the "mystery" which some young people face about sex is not knowing what happens during sexual activity. Actually, it is difficult to explain in a general way, since each individual must learn at some point what sex is all about for himself or herself. I shall try, however, to describe what may happen as clearly as possible. To understand this section fully, be certain that you have read about male and female anatomy in Chapter Two and about the sexual response cycle in Chapter Three.

### Foreplay

Preceding the period of heightened sexual activity leading to orgasm, the couple usually spends some time deepening their levels of sexual sharing. Typically, that begins with kissing, caressing, and petting. These activities lead to sexual excitement in both partners. You will remember that sexual excitement is characterized by erection of the penis in males and secretion of liquid along the inner walls of the vagina in females. The period before attempting orgasm is often referred to as "foreplay" and may last only a few minutes or for a much longer time. During that time, the degree of sexual arousal in both partners may increase and decrease several times.

### Mutual Masturbation

Part of the period of foreplay usually includes touching of the partner's sexual organs, and such touching may also lead to orgasm by means of mutual masturbation (see Chapter Three). Although this way of reaching orgasm is most common among young people who are experimenting with sex, or among those who wish to avoid other forms of sexual activity for some reason, some couples continue to enjoy mutual masturbation to orgasm throughout an extended relationship. It may be used as a way of varying their sexual activity.

### Sexual Intercourse

A common form of sexual activity for heterosexual couples is sexual intercourse, or coitus, which refers to the insertion of a man's penis into a woman's vagina. This insertion may take a little time and some gentle effort, depending on the size of the vagina and the amount of lubrication. If the woman has not experienced intercourse before and the hymen is still present, the penis may rupture the hymen, and the woman *may* experience some mild discomfort and a small amount of bleeding (see page 23).

After the penis is comfortably inside the vagina, the two partners move rhythmically in ways which give both pleasant sensations. Usually, both partners move their pelvises in a way that moves the penis in and out of the vagina. These pelvic movements may be varied from slow and gentle rhythms to rapid, vigorous thrusting. Which partner controls the movements and the rate depends partly on the position of the two people. Sexual intercourse may take place in a great variety of positions. Couples often enjoy experimenting to find the positions which are most comfortable and enjoyable for them. One of the myths that we often hear wild stories about is that the vagina sometimes contracts so the penis becomes caught inside, and the two people are unable to separate. This is completely untrue and does not occur. Because male dogs have a different penis structure than humans, they do become temporarily "caught" during mating, but this is an important part of successful breeding in dogs.

During intercourse, the bodies of both the male and female usually go through all of the expected phases of the sexual response cycle: excitement, plateau, orgasm, and resolution. Males nearly always reach orgasm during intercourse, and since they then usually lose their erections, intercourse is finished for them until after the refractory period has ended. Some females do not reach orgasm each time they have intercourse. For some women, this is a real concern while for others it apparently does not matter. Some women also have more than one orgasm during intercourse. Women may want to continue intercourse after reaching orgasm since they have no refractory period and do not have to maintain an erection. This is not to say, however, that women should not play a part in deciding when intercourse should continue or when it should cease. It should be noted that most people at one time or another experience some problems in having sexual intercourse. Some typical problems are discussed in Chapter Seven.

### Oral Sex

Oral sexual contact means using the mouth or tongue to touch or stimulate another person's sex organs. It can involve taking the male penis into the mouth or using the tongue to stimulate the female clitoris or vagina. The mouth may also be used to stimulate other sensitive areas of the body, including both male and female nipples. Although oral stimulation may be used as a prelude to other sexual activity leading to orgasm, it is also a common way of achieving orgasm for both males and females.

It would appear from the studies of sex researchers that a majority of people find oral sexual contact to be pleasurable and acceptable. Others find the idea of oral sex disgusting or immoral. Like so many other aspects of sexual behavior, this is often an area that partners must discuss with one another and come to some mutual decisions about. One partner should not be coerced into any sexual activity against his or her will. When basic rules of cleanliness and hygiene are observed in the mouth as well as in the sex organs, there seem to be no special medical dangers associated with oral sexual contact.

### Anal Sex

Anal sex refers to the insertion of the male penis into the anus of his partner. It is a form of sexual behavior that may sometimes be shared by male homosexuals and by heterosexual couples. Unlike the vagina, the anus does not have its own source of lubrication, thus great gentleness and care must be taken, and a lubricating substance is often necessary for insertion. Because bacteria live in the rectum, the penis should not be inserted in the vagina or mouth following anal insertion, without being washed first. As with oral sex, some people find anal sex to be immoral and disgusting. However, unless there are special medical problems or diseases present, when cleanliness and care are observed, there are no special medical dangers associated with anal sexual contact. It is believed that the disease AIDS may be spread from an infected person through anal intercourse.

### After Sex

The length of time spent in sexual activity leading to orgasm varies with different couples and different situations. It is obvious that one of the common time-determining factors is the length of time it takes to reach orgasm. In any case, such activity may last less than a minute or for much longer periods of time, even up to an hour or more. Again, both partners should cooperate in finding the length of time that is best for each of them, and that may vary at different times.

Most couples find that the togetherness before and after orgasm is very important for the expression of warm, loving feelings toward one another. Not only may sexual activity help an individual feel that his or her body is desirable and cared for, it may also lead to a strengthening of the total relationship. It is not, however, a substitute for the real work of making a meaningful relationship, nor is it an adequate way of solving the real problems that arise when two people are trying to be important to each other.

### Sex and Your Values

Until recent years, one of the predominant values of American society was that a couple should not engage in sexual activity outside of marriage. Many people did not abide by that value, however, and some of them felt very guilty about not doing so. There are still many religious groups and individuals who feel that sexual activity outside of marriage is morally wrong. There are others who believe that marriage and religious convictions are not the issues, but that sex outside of a responsible, committed relationship in which there is love and caring, is ultimately unrewarding.

There has been another attitude about sex in our society for many years. It is also present in many other societies. This is the view that young men are more apt to have casual sexual experiences than are young women. In a variety of ways—through the media, their peers, and sometimes their parents—boys are led to believe that casual sex is not only all right for them, but that there is something wrong with them if they don't have it. Yet, the same is not true for girls. Instead, messages are conveyed to them that "nice" girls not only do not have casual sex, but that they don't have any desire for it. This whole confusing, unfair set of values is called the *double standard*. There are, of course, many other double standards for males and females, many of them as equally absurd. Take, for example, the idea that it is all right for girls to touch and kiss each other as ways of showing tenderness and affection, but that is not all right for boys.

Within the past three decades, attitudes and values about sex have been changing. That is not to say that many people now do not feel that sexual activity outside of marriage is wrong. They do. However, many others believe that marriage in itself should not be the "justification" for sex. Instead, these people believe it is the quality of the relationship and the maturity of the two people in it which should determine whether sexual activity is the "right" step.

Like most other decisions about sex, whether or not to engage in sexual activity, either outside of marriage or outside of a committed relationship, will have to be *your* decision. Although on the surface it may seem to be a simple decision, there may be many issues which deserve careful consideration. For example, it will probably be necessary for you to weigh into your decision the moral values of your parents, religious teachings, community, peers, and of your potential sex partner. As I stated earlier, while sex carries with it extreme pleasure and joy, it also has the potential for hurting ourselves and others. I have talked with many young people who have been emotionally hurt to some degree by sex, usually because they have not had adequate opportunities to figure out what they want before becoming deeply involved with sex. I have also talked with many people who have found sex to be a happy bond in their relationships. In the following section, I hope you will consider the possible consequences—positive and negative—of embarking on sexual experiences.

### Deciding About Sex

Making the decision about whether or not to have sex outside of marriage used to be simpler when society's values were more clearcut. As one of my students once said, "Even if you did it, at least you didn't have to worry about whether you were right or wrong. You knew you were wrong!" It would be easier if I could just list all the right reasons and all the wrong reasons for you, but that cannot be done. In fact, it is impossible for me to generalize about the consequences of sex. I can only describe what some of the *possible* consequences could be. Think about each of them and how each might fit for your life.

First, let's take a look at some possible negative consequences:

1. *Unwanted Pregnancy.*   This is always a possibility any time intercourse takes place. Birth control methods (see Chapter Ten) reduce the risks of pregnancy, but they cannot eliminate them completely. If an unwanted pregnancy occurs, very difficult decisions must be faced concerning alternative routes of action: abortion, adoption, marriage, or single parenthood. The problem of an unwanted pregnancy may occur in marriage as well as before.

2. *Unexpected Emotional Involvement.*   Even casual sexual activity often produces intense emotional reactions, even if those reactions are not wanted. Intimate physical contact sometimes generates strong emotional attachments which may be difficult for both partners to cope with. For some young people, sexual activity is mistakenly interpreted as a sign of long-lasting commitment to the relationship. This is simply another reason why good communication between people is so essential *before* sex takes place.

3. *Guilt and Regret.*   Let's face it: plenty of people still feel guilty and regretful about sexual experiences, especially if they are violating moral codes of their parents or their religion. Guilt doesn't help young persons to feel good about themselves and may eventually be quite destructive. Each individual must carefully consider the potential of sex producing guilt in his or her life, and attempt to pursue relationships which will not be regretted later.

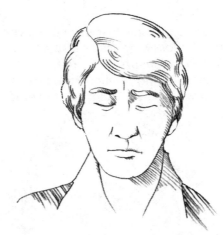

4. *Feeling "Conned" or Used.* Sexual activity that is positive and healthy takes place as a matter of choice in an atmosphere of mutual honesty and trust. It is unfortunate that some people—both males and females—view the persuasion of another person into sex as some sort of "conquest," or as a way to "hold on" to the other person. Not only are these poor reasons for sexual activity, but it is almost inevitable that the other partner will eventually feel as if he or she has been "conned" and used.

5. *Possibility of Disease.* The incidence of venereal disease, or V.D., is on the rise. These are diseases transmitted by sexual contact, and are now called sexually transmitted diseases (or STDs). They are discussed in more detail in Chapter Seven. If a sexual partner is chosen who has shared sex with someone else, there may be a risk that he or she has a sexually transmitted disease. Although treatment is available for STD, some young people are too embarrassed to seek medical help. As unfortunate as it may seem, this factor must also be considered when making decisions about sex.

Now, we may consider some of the possible positive consequences of sexual activity. Some of these benefits may be derived even in casual sex, but it should be emphasized that positive consequences are generally possible only in the context of a loving, committed relationship between the two people involved.

You should also keep in mind that sexual activity is *only one of the ways in which the following may be achieved:*

1. *Learning the Pleasure of Sexual Sharing.* In the context of a healthy, loving relationship, sexual activity can often provide new heights of physical and emotional pleasure.

2. *Feeling Good About Your Body.* When we get pleasure from our bodies while giving another person pleasure, we often feel more positively about what our bodies have to offer. Additionally, when we feel that our body is attractive and sexually desirable to another, we generally feel good about it.

3. *Deepening the Sense of Intimacy and Caring.* In a relationship that involves real intimacy and caring, sexual activity can be an expression of these feelings, and can deepen them. If the relationship is the one of giving and getting it should be, then sexual activity can symbolize this relationship, and both partners may feel more closely involved than ever before.

4. *Learning About Sexual Functioning.* Many individuals learn a great deal about their body's sexual responsiveness during shared sexual activity. Some girls and women do not experience orgasm until they have had sexual experience with another person. There are studies which show that premarital intercourse can lead to more rapid sexual adjust-

ment after marriage, though not necessarily a better adjustment. Some people in committed relationships report that they are glad of having had previous sexual experience, while others regret such experience and feel that it was not helpful to them.

5. *Learning About Sexual Responsibility.* Some young people report that previous sexual experience helped them to learn about the responsibilities they must take in deeper, more committed relationships. Often, they report that they have learned by making some mistakes with sex. Since most people know how "mistakes" with sex may so strongly affect lives, they hope that others will make as few mistakes as possible. Yet, maybe the most important suggestions I can give you are to try to prevent mistakes by thinking carefully about your decisions and to learn whatever you can from your own mistakes or those of others.

**Not Having Sex**

The facts are that many young people—even those involved in long-term relationships—are not having sex. We live in pressured times sexually, and sometimes it is difficult to keep in mind that *it is okay not to have sex.* Plenty of young people who take the time to think through their decisions and to discuss sex with their partners decide that sexual activity will have to be postponed, until later. Not having sex is sometimes called *abstinence.* Some couples decide to give one another sexual pleasure through petting, while others limit themselves to less intense levels of sharing such as kissing and hugging.

It should also be noted that neither marriage nor any other form of committed relationship insures a great sexual relationship. Sexual problems and frustrations are commonly brought to marriage counselors and sex therapists. In a relationship where the two people are truly committed to one another and want to improve their sexual sharing, sex may usually be improved and made to be much less of a problem.

It is not a simple matter to make decisions about sex. Often, there is downright confusion and misunderstanding. Hopefully, the exercises at the end of this chapter will help you to think through your values on these issues.

### More Than Two

Some people—married and unmarried—become involved in sharing sexual experiences with more than one other participant present. This may mean two or more couples being sexually involved separately in the same room, or it may mean three or more people touching each other in sexual ways, including intercourse. The research studies on such sexual experiences are limited at this point. It may well be that some individuals find sex with more than one other person enjoyable and interesting. However, there is also evidence that many people do not adjust well to group sex experiences and that jealousy may become a big problem for some. In any case, it is obvious that the more people involved in a sexual experience, the more complicated responsible decision-making will inevitably become.

### Are You Ready?

If you come to a point in your life when you are interested in sharing sex with another person, you may want to consider the following areas. They are things that should be thought about and that you might want to discuss with your potential partner:

1.  What do you expect from your partner in the way of love and caring, and what does your partner expect of you? Check any of the following which apply to the directions your relationship seems to be taking:

    _____ We love each other.

    _____ We're trying to understand what love means to us.

    _____ We're good friends, but not in love.

    _____ We probably won't ever be married, but we are working on a committed relationship.

    _____ We expect to be married when that is possible in a practical sense.

    _____ We have already begun marriage plans.

    _____ I sometimes am not certain if he/she cares about me as much as I care back.

    _____ I feel pressured to have sex, even though I'm not sure I'm ready.

    _____ We've already done a lot of petting, but we are postponing more serious sex until we are more ready.

_____ We've already had some intense sex together, but we're not sure we want to again right away.

_____ We have intercourse regularly, and plan to continue to do so.

_____ We do not plan to have intercourse until after we're married.

_____ I sometimes don't think that he/she enjoys sexual contact as much as I do.

_____ I sometimes worry about possible pregnancy.

2. The following is a list of what most professionals consider to be poor reasons in themselves for having sex with another person. Think carefully about whether or not any of them *could be* your reasons or your partner's:

    a. To improve the relationship
    b. To prove that you are a responsible adult
    c. To feel independent from parents
    d. To rebel against traditional values
    e. To show that you really love the other person
    f. To go along with what others seem to be doing
    g. To prove that you're good at sex

3. Are you ready to accept possible negative consequences such as an unwanted pregnancy? Are you able to discuss the issue of birth control with your partner? What form of birth control have you decided to use and have you investigated its effectiveness (see Chapter Ten)?

4. If you decide to share sexual activity, how much deceit will be involved? Are you going to have to lie to your parents or others about where you are going, and—if so—how do you feel about lying?

5. Have you weighed into the decision the moral values of your parents? your religion? your school and community? your peers? your partner?

6. Make a list—in writing—of what your goals would be in having sex with someone. Have your partner make such a list too. When both lists are finished, get together, compare them, and talk about what you have learned. Sound crazy? Maybe, but it's worth a try.

7. Consider the following spectrum of possible sexual values. Try to locate on each line whether you fall at one extreme or the other, or whether you consider yourself somewhere in between:

I would have sex
with anyone I could
persuade into it.

I would have sex if
we really cared about
each other and both
chose to.

I would have sex only
with a person whom I
love very much and
with whom I have a
long-term relationship.

Premarital sex is all
right under any
circumstances.

Premarital intercourse
is ok for some and not
so good for others,
depending on the
maturity of the couple.

No one should have
sexual intercourse
until after marriage.

## For Further Reading

Calderone, Mary S. and Johnson, Eric W. *The Family Book About Sexuality*. New York: Harper and Row, 1981.

Gordon, Sol. *You Would if You Loved Me*. New York: Bantam, 1979.

Mazur, Ronald M. *Commonsense Sex*. Boston: Beacon Press, 1973.

Planned Parenthood. *Sexuality . . . Decisions, Attitudes, Relationships* (booklet). Philadelphia: Planned Parenthood of Southeastern Pennsylvania, 1979.

Pomeroy, Wardell. *Boys and Sex*. New York: Delacorte Press, 1981.

Pomeroy, Wardell. *Girls and Sex*. New York: Delacorte Press, 1981.

# 6   Communicating About Sex

We hear a great deal lately about the importance of good communication in human relationships. As a counselor who talks with other people about their feelings and concerns, I must be continually aware of how important good communication really is. Yet, I have also discovered that many individuals have a great deal of misunderstanding about how to establish lines of communication.

I have come to believe that there are three important foundations which must be established before people can communicate with each other with full effectiveness. Those three foundations are as follows:

1. *A Sense of Equality.* Both individuals must feel a sense of equality as human beings and as good worthwhile people. There cannot be an underlying belief that one person is "better" than the other. Little productive two-way communication can take place if one of the individuals feels judged, put-down, or preached at by the other. Such feelings often lead to defensiveness and pointless argument. So, for effective communication to take place, both people must be willing to be open to the other's ideas, opinions, and feelings, even though there may be disagreement over them. It is important to remember that people communicate in different ways. One partner in a relationship, for example, may have a better capacity to find the truth in a situation and clarify the scope of a problem. The other partner may more

easily discover the right thing to do in a situation, and put decisions into action. Equality in a relationship doesn't mean that
people have only the same things to contribute.

2. *The Desire to Communicate.* Not much is going to
happen either unless both people really want to communicate.
If fear, stubbornness, lack of caring, or some other block gets in
the way of one person's desire to communicate, it is not likely
that much is going to happen. There are many reasons why people may desire to communicate. Among those reasons are a desire to improve the relationship; inner discomforts which need to
be talked out; tension between the two people to be dealt with;
or simply knowing the joy that real communication may yield.

3. *Working at it.* Good two-way communication takes energy. It is always a bit risky because sharing openly with another
person leaves us more vulnerable than before. So, work—ex-
penditure of energy—is necessary. Like any other kind of work,
we sometimes have to make the effort to communicate even
when we're not quite in the mood.

I hope that these three foundations do not seem overwhelm-
ing to you. However, the unavoidable fact is that good communication between human beings is not a simple matter; it doesn't
"just happen." It grows out of human foundations.

### What Gets Communicated and How?

We should now look at the elements of communication. In
other words, what kinds of things get communicated from person
to person? Here is a list of some of the most important elements
of communication:

1. Thoughts and ideas
2. Feelings
3. Values, attitudes, and opinions
4. Needs and desires

All of these things may be communicated to another person.
They are conveyed in a great variety of ways, some of the most
common of which follow:

1. *Using Words.* A great deal of communication occurs
through the use of words, either spoken or on paper.

2. *Eye Contact.* It is said that the eyes are the mirrors of

the soul. There certainly can be some important messages communicated by the amount of eye contact two people have.

3. *Facial Expression.* Our faces are particularly important in communication. Even when we hear words from another individual, we often scan his or her face, searching for the true meaning behind the words.

4. *Body Movements and Contact.* The manner in which our body moves also conveys messages to others. A particularly intense form of communication involves one person physically touching another.

## Misunderstandings and Games

A big problem with communication is that one person often does not fully understand the other person's exact meaning. Or, the meaning may be completely misinterpreted. This is one of the reasons why good communication takes so much work. It is essential to stay really in touch with what another person is saying and sometimes we have to ask questions in order to understand the whole message. Often, we are too busy thinking about what we ourselves are going to say next to really listen.

Sometimes people substitute games and deceptions for good communication. Getting caught up in games can happen easily, and some individuals find it simpler to play the game than to strive for open, honest, two-way communication. For more selfish reasons, communication may also become deceitful manipulation of another person. This is a dangerous kind of communication since it is almost certain to produce further misunderstandings and hurt.

## Sex and Communication

One of the very important areas about which people often need to communicate is sexuality. Most of what we learn about sex is communicated to us by other people. Yet sex is also an area that creates feelings which can block good communication. When the subject of sex comes up, some people feel embarrassed, ashamed, afraid, or even angry. Instead of being able to communicate those feelings, they may try to avoid the whole subject. Some individuals also hold very strong values and attitudes about sex and do not care to hear from others who might not agree with them. Consequently, sex often just doesn't get talked about.

There is one important suggestion that I often give to people who want to improve lines of communication about sex (or anything) with someone else. It is to try to present honestly just *what you are feeling.* We can really only guess what is going on with the other person anyway, so it is dangerous to make assumptions. Sometimes, it is even difficult to know exactly what we ourselves are feeling. Here is an illustration of some poor communication, showing what is really going on and also how the communication could have been improved by being honest about feelings:

| *What was said:* | *What was being thought:* | *What could have been said:* |
|---|---|---|
| Ed: "I heard you went out with Rick last night." | (How come you didn't call me last night?) | "I was kind of hoping we could go somewhere together last night, but I heard you went out with Rick." |
| Sue: "Yeah, Ann and I went to the movies, and Rick happened to be there too. So he sat with us." | (I wonder why he sounds so mad? How come he didn't call me if he wanted to see me so much?) | "I was hoping you would call me. But then Ann called and we went to the movies. Rick just happened to sit with us." |
| Ed: (sarcastically) "Did you have a good time?" | (Maybe she enjoyed being with him more than she would have with me.) | "When I heard you were with him, I felt really kind of hurt and confused." |
| Sue: (defensively) "So what if I did? I have a right to do what I want to do." | (Doesn't he trust me?) | "I'm sorry you were hurt. I guess we both should have tried to get together last night." |
| Ed: "I thought we were going steady." | (I'm afraid I'm losing her.) | "Probably. But sometimes I worry that you are getting sick of having me around." |
| Sue: "That doesn't mean you own me." | (Sometimes he makes me feel so trapped!) | "I'm not sick of you at all. I worry about the same thing. But maybe sometimes we need to spend time apart. That doesn't mean we care about each other less." |

Ed: (angrily) "Well, if you want to break up, just tell me."

(I don't want this to happen, but maybe she's sick of me.)

"Yeah, but sometimes I get scared of losing you."

Sue: (frustrated) "That's not what I meant."

(Why does he always bring that up? Probably he's the one who wants to break up.)

"I don't even like to think about breaking up with you."

The kind of communication which Ed and Sue exhibited is not unusual. It is typical of the misunderstandings and second-guessing games which go on between people all the time. Yet, this poor communication may be turned into positive, productive communication by remembering to stop second-guessing the other person and to share your own thoughts and feelings to the greatest extent you feel able. To be sure, that kind of openness leaves us vulnerable, and some people take advantage of others' vulnerability. But most will respond by sharing their thoughts and feelings, and then two-way communication is underway.

### Talking with Parents About Sex

When it comes to sex, don't sell your parents short. Keep in mind that they are sexual people too and may have many worthwhile things to share with you. Some parents find it easy to talk with their kids about sex, while others are extremely uncomfortable with the subject. If you're interested in their ideas and values concerning sexuality, it may be up to you to initiate the discussion. It is also good to remember that very little may be accomplished if the discussion turns into an argument. When there is disagreement, it is best to try to see the other's point of view and try to understand it as *different*, not wrong. The same rules for productive communication apply in families too. Instead of second-guessing what the other person is feeling and thinking, try to convey as honestly as possible what *you* are feeling and thinking. With parents, as well as others with whom you attempt to communicate, it's important to know when to stop trying to communicate. If values and attitudes are set, and unlikely to change, it may sometimes be best just to accept this.

## Sex Education

In recent years, there have been many controversies about sex education. Actually, sex education of one sort or another goes on around us all the time. It begins when we are born. From the moment we are assigned our status as boy or girl, we are taught to think and act about our sexuality in very specific ways. We are sometimes dressed in blue or pink and given toys considered appropriate for boys or girls. As we progress through childhood, we learn many attitudes toward our bodies and sex from our parents. Usually by late childhood, we have learned to feel positively or negatively about our sex organs and our sexual feelings.

Our families are one of our most important sources of sex education, even into adulthood. Our peers—people our own age—often are significant sources of information about sex. More and more, schools and religious groups are offering sex education programs to young people and sometimes to adults. A full program in sex education consists of two aspects: 1) facts about our bodies and how they function sexually (this is what I usually call the "plumbing") and 2) opportunity to talk about sexual feelings and values with peers.

Sex education in public schools must allow for a free exchange of facts and values, rather than adherence to a single point of view. Church or synagogue programs are legitimate places for the teaching of particular religious or moral values concerning sex. Parents, too, usually want to convey to their children the moral values in which they believe. If you ever become a parent, some of the responsibility for educating your children about sex will be yours.

Sex education is a lifelong process. Throughout our lives we continue to learn about our own sexuality and about the facts of sex. There are many books now available and many more yet to appear that can help people to understand human sexuality more fully. Choose your books with care, however, and beware of those which promise to erase effortlessly all of your sexual concerns and inhibitions.

### Communication and Healthy Sexual Relationships

One of the most dangerous areas for games, deceptions, and misunderstandings is sex. In a healthy, growing relationship where sexual feelings are involved in any way, communication may be of extreme importance. Attention must continually be given to what is going on between two people sexually: Is one person feeling guilty, or trapped, or inadequate? Is sex being used as an escape or a cover-up of negative feelings? Are both partners happy and satisfied with what they are doing sexually?

Earlier in this Chapter, there was an example of some poor communication between Ed and Sue as they discussed their relationship. The same kinds of mis-communication can happen when two people talk about sex. Here is how Ed and Sue tried to communicate about sex in their relationship.

| *What was said:* | *What was being thought:* | *What could have been said:* |
|---|---|---|
| Sue: "Whenever we're alone, you're all over me." | (Sometimes I think he only enjoys being with me when we're alone.) | "I really need to talk about how I feel when we're alone like this." |
| Ed: (sarcastically) "I suppose you don't like it." | (What's going on? I thought this is what she wanted me to do.) | (curiously) "Okay, what's going on?" |
| Sue: "What's that supposed to mean—I'm easy?" | (I wonder what he *does* think about me.) | "I've just been wondering how you feel about me lately. Sometimes I think you just like being with me for sex." |
| Ed: "Everybody else is doing it. Why shouldn't we?" | (What's wrong with her all of a sudden?) | "I've been feeling kind of the same way. I'm confused about the whole thing." |

| *What was said:* | *What was being thought:* | *What could have been said:* |
|---|---|---|
| Sue: "Is that all I am? Another conquest to brag about to your friends?" | (Sometimes he makes me feel so used.) | "I guess we never thought very much about what sex would mean to us." |
| Ed: "If that's what you think, I guess you don't know me very well." | (I thought she knew how we felt about each other.) | "It means a lot to me, but nothing is more important than how we feel toward each other." |
| Sue: "No, I guess I don't anymore, since we started having sex." | (I don't think he cares about me anymore except for sex.) | "I'm glad you feel that way too." |

Good communication about sex also takes honesty and openness about feelings. When two people can avoid accusations, and can share fears, needs, and concerns instead, there is a much greater likelihood that they will improve their sexual relationship rather than harm it.

Another essential part of a healthy sexual relationship is compromise. Neither partner can have things exactly his or her own way all the time. There must be compromises in both directions, and there cannot be meaningful compromise without good communication and mutual caring. Both people must share thoughts, feelings, preferences, and needs, and then care enough about one another to find the kind of sexual sharing that will be enjoyable, fulfilling, satisfying, and fair to both.

Many sexual problems can develop when lines of communication break down between the two partners or when one person is no longer willing to compromise. When tensions or worries build up inside an individual because of sex, it may be a good time to find someone to talk to. The next section discusses important ways to find a counselor.

### Finding a Counselor
To whom do you talk when you have a problem or have something you need to think through with another person? Whether it is to talk about sex or any other aspect of our lives, most of us sometimes feel the need to share some thoughts and

feelings with another person. Perhaps you already know who that person would be for your life: a parent, a brother or sister, a counselor, a teacher, a member of the clergy, your best friend, a grandparent, or another relative. But what happens if you just don't know whom you should choose? What kind of individual do you search for? I shall try to explain some of the things that seem to be important for me and many other people in finding someone to talk with.

First, be careful not to look for someone to solve your problems for you or make decisions for you. If you take time to think and feel and talk about what is going on, you will be able to find your own directions for your life. So look for someone who will not be too anxious to jump in and run things for you; someone who will be able to give you the freedom and responsibility to live your own life while giving you support, understanding, and the new perspective that another human being may have to offer. I wish I could say that if you seek out a counselor or doctor or psychologist you will automatically find such a person, but this is not always the case. Professional qualifications do not guarantee the presence of the "right" personal qualities which you may need in another. Likewise, many individuals without special training may be very good people to share things with.

Here are some of the qualities you might want to have in a person with whom you are going to talk:

1. *Trust.* It is always important to feel trust for the person, knowing that what you talk about will be held in confidence and that your best interests will be foremost in that person's mind.

2. *Respect.* Most people prefer to talk with others whose own lives seem worthy of respect. Although we cannot expect perfection from others, I usually appreciate talking with someone who is always working at being happy and at getting things straight for his or her own life.

3. *Caring.* How important it is to know that the other person can really care for you enough to want to share some thoughts and feelings with you! If he or she does not take your concerns very seriously, then look for someone who will.

4. *No quick judgements.* It seems that we make the best progress when the other person is not too quick to make judgements about what is going on. Look for a good listener who can sift through all aspects of the situation with you without coming to any quick conclusions or instant solutions.

5. *Empathy.* This refers to the ability to understand what other people are really feeling and being able to some degree to feel it along with them. It is an essential quality for a good counselor.

6. *Genuineness.* It is important for most people to talk with someone who is willing to share some of his or her own life as well; someone who will care enough to show feelings and thoughts, even if they are not quite what we might "want to hear." Yet, it is important that any sharing is done in a real spirit of caring.

7. *Understanding.* We need to talk with people who will work to understand what we mean as closely as possible. With so much opportunity for misunderstanding in human communication, good counselors are always making certain that they understand what is being said to the best of their abilities.

How you might go about finding the right person for you to talk with will have to be up to you. It is always possible to ask someone you trust to suggest a good counselor for you, but the final decision should be your own. Some of the organizations listed on pages 187–188, or their local affiliates, may be able to offer some help. If you are talking with someone you did not know beforehand, it may take more than one session before you can be certain whether or not this is the right person for you. Remember: it is usually scary to take that first step—to talk over some deeply personal things with someone else, especially if you do not know that person well.

Don't expect counselors to pick things out of your head. They too have to rely on honest, open communication to understand what is going on with another person. If you have spent some time talking with a counselor, really working at sharing yourself with him or her, and you still feel uncomfortable, then it would be wise to tell the counselor how you are feeling. Good counselors will help you to sort through your feelings so that you feel more comfortable talking with them or they will help you find someone else who is better for you. Keep in mind that you have the right to look for another counselor if you have not found the right one for yourself.

### Communication and You
1.  *Letters to Mom and Dad.*
    a. Here are two letters which young people gave me when I asked them to write what they would like to be able to tell their parents. Their parents never actually read the letters, and the two teenagers never got around to talking these things over with them. Read the two letters carefully and think about them. How do you feel about the people who wrote them? Do they sound at all like things you would like to tell your parents?

> Dear Mom and Dad,
>     There are so many things I wish I could tell you. For one thing, why don't you trust me anymore? You don't seem to like some of my friends very much, but I don't really think you have given yourselves a chance to get to know them. They're good kids, really!
>     Sometimes, I lie to you about what I'm doing. When I tell you I'm going to the library or the movies, I'm usually riding around with some kids or hanging around a dorm at the college. I don't do anything wrong, but if I told you the truth, you would probably think the worst. I hate lying to you, but I don't know what else to do. Please try to understand me at least a little.
>                                             Your daughter,
>                                             Marie   (age 16)

> Dear Mom and Dad,
>     There is only one way to start this—just jump in. I want to talk to you about sex. That's right: S-E-X. I've never heard much about it from you, but I've managed

to find out quite a bit for myself. I started masturbating seven years ago, and I've already had intercourse a few times.

The thing is, I still don't know what I want with sex. So far, it hasn't been too great, and it has hurt a lot of feelings. Sometimes, I even worry that I might be a little queer. So I need to talk about sex, and I don't know how. I feel like I have a lot more to learn. Can you help?

Your confused son,
Sam   (age 16)

b.  Now, try writing your own "Dear Mom and Dad" letter. Sit down with a piece of paper and write those things that you would like to say to them. Perhaps there is someone else to whom you would like to write a letter. Give that a try also. Remember, you don't have to send the letter.

2.   *Dealing with Anger.*
Try to recall the last two or three times when you got angry with another person. Remember the incidents in as much detail as possible, then consider the following aspects of each incident:

a.  How did you express your anger? Did you yell, fight, cry, or sulk? Did you store it up inside and pretend you weren't angry?

b.  Now, try to look beneath your anger. Is there a possibility that the other person *hurt* you in some way? Very often, when our feelings get hurt, we react with anger. How might you have been hurt?

c.  If you were hurt, try to imagine what might have happened if you had told the other person that he or she hurt you, instead of getting angry. Could that have worked for you and perhaps even strengthened your relationship with that person?

d.  Next time you begin to feel anger, try to stop and take a look at what you are really feeling. Try to share that with the other person and talk out what you both feel. It may be a step toward productive communication. (It is difficult to talk when you are really angry, though, so ironing out problems may sometimes have to wait until you've calmed down. Also, if a person you are trying to deal with *always* seems to get angry, or to make you angry, that may be a sign that he or she is a person you just cannot communicate with.)

3.  *Communication and Sex.*
       a.  Here is a list of topics relating to sex which may concern you in some way. Check which people you feel able to talk with about each topic at this point in your life (you may want to use a separate paper):

*I can talk about this with:*

| Topics | A Parent | A Brother or Sister | A Good Friend | No One |
|---|---|---|---|---|
| Masturbation | ____ | ____ | ____ | ____ |
| Sexual intercourse | ____ | ____ | ____ | ____ |
| Homosexuality | ____ | ____ | ____ | ____ |
| My sexual feelings | ____ | ____ | ____ | ____ |
| My body and sex organs | ____ | ____ | ____ | ____ |
| What I have done sexually | ____ | ____ | ____ | ____ |
| My sexual worries | ____ | ____ | ____ | ____ |
| Premarital sex | ____ | ____ | ____ | ____ |

b.  Now, look at your check marks. Are there more check marks in some columns than others? What do your marks tell you about your relationship with others?

c.  Are you satisfied with the patterns which your check marks have taken? Would you like to improve your communication with other people about sex? If so, begin to think about how you might accomplish that. It may be easier than you think. It may also be harder than you think, especially if the other person is not ready to meet you half way. Remember, *both* parties must be willing to communicate, and it's important to choose people who are as willing to be open as you are.

## For Further Reading

Bell, Ruth. *Changing Bodies, Changing Lives: A Book for Teens on Sex and Relationships.* New York: Random House, 1981.

Brenton, Myron. *Sex Talk.* Briarcliff Manor, NY: Stein and Day, 1977.

Gordon, Sol. *Psychology for You.* Fayetteville, NY (P.O. Box 583): Ed-U-Press, 1981.

Gordon, Sol. *The Teenage Survival Book.* Fayetteville, NY (P.O. Box 583): Ed-U-Press, 1981.

Hamilton, Eleanor. *Sex with Love: A Guide for Young People.* Boston: Beacon Press, 1978.

Johnson, Eric W. *Sex: Telling it Straight* (an easily read book). New York: Harper and Row, 1979.

Kramer, Patricia. *The Dynamics of Relationships.* Kensington, MD: Equal Partners, 1985.

# 7    Problem Sex

When does sex become a problem? It may be a problem in many different ways for many different people. It is probably safe to assume that almost all people have a sex-related problem or concern at some time in their lives. Such problems may last for a lifetime if not dealt with adequately, or they may disappear easily after a very short time.

There are several ways in which sexual feelings or activities may become a problem. Here are some of those ways:

1)   When they produce guilt, fear, or negative attitudes about oneself.

2)   When another person's right to privacy is violated or a law is broken.

3)   When one person does not consider personal responsibility toward another and uses sexual deception or manipulation.

4)   When someone is emotionally or physically harmed by the feelings or activities.

5)   When the body does not function as expected or desired.

6)   When an unwanted pregnancy occurs. (See Chapter Ten)

7)   When a disease is transmitted by the sexual contact.

## What People Worry About

As a counselor and sex therapist, I have talked with many individuals about their sexual worries. Some of those individuals mistakenly believed that they were the *only* ones who have had their particular worry. Actually, their concerns are usually quite typical. That does not make the problem any less troublesome, however. One of the most common worries is about *bodily development.* Boys and men often dislike their general physical appearance or believe their penises to be undersized. Sometimes, they are embarrassed enough to avoid swimming or other situations where they might be even partially unclothed. Likewise, girls and women are particularly prone to worry about their breast development, as well as general physical appearance.

*Masturbation* is another typical concern of people at all ages. People often wonder if they are masturbating too much or what the effects of masturbation may be. Usually accurate information can clear up many of these worries and doubts. Masturbation was discussed in detail in Chapter Three. Young people also worry about the *daydreams* and *fantasies* they may have while masturbating or just thinking about sex. They sometimes fear that their fantasies mean that they are "weird." Actually, most people occasionally think about some sexual practices which they may choose never to become involved in. For example, it is not unusual to daydream about sexual involvement with another person of either sex, such as a brother or sister, a teacher, or a stranger who is sexually attractive. You do not have to do what you think about. It will be up to you to decide whether doing any of the things you daydream about corresponds with your basic preferences and values.

Many young people who become involved in close relationships find their sexual worries increasing if they begin dating or sharing loving feelings. Both boys and girls wonder if they should initiate sex play with their dating partners and wonder how to go about making such advances. Early attempts at sexual contact may be awkward and embarrassing, and that only leads to further worry. If sex play is begun, then there may be further concern about *"how far to go."* If the relationship begins to involve intensive sexual activity, then it is possible for many new problems to develop, several of which have been described in Chapter Five. Many people face *guilt* or other negative feelings after sex, and following heterosexual intercourse, there is often a *fear of pregnancy*. Another common concern is that one has *too much or too little* "sex drive," or that one is not *"performing"* in sex as well as possible. Later in this chapter, several problems with sexual functioning are discussed.

Those young people who become involved in relationships with members of their same sex may find their sexual worries increasing. They not only have the same problems in making relationships and knowing when sex is appropriate, but other worries as well. They may have loving feelings for people whom they would not dare tell. They may have to hide the fact that they are "dating" or experimenting with sex. Though many colleges and some high schools now have gay social organizations, and some larger communities have gay youth groups, gay young people often have a difficult time finding ways to meet other gay people in a congenial setting that is suitable for building relationships. Due to the attitudes in our society about homosexuality, young people who embark on homosexual relationships may have even greater problems with guilt. Young men and women who are experiencing guilt about homosexual feelings must ask themselves whether or not this guilt is justified by their own values and life-style choices. It may be desirable to talk over such concerns with a counselor (see Chapter Six). If you would like to find out more about gay organizations in your area, you might contact one of the organizations listed in Appendix II.

So these concerns represent very typical sexual worries of human beings. There are no magic solutions or easy answers that will make such worries disappear. Each of us must sort through his or her own conflicts, feelings, and values, searching for the life-style and sexuality which fit best. Sometimes, it helps to talk over our worries with a trusted person, as we discussed in the last chapter.

The next few sections of this chapter describe some other sex-related problems which people may face, some of which may be quite serious.

## Sex and Handicaps

People with physical handicaps often have their own special sex-related problems. Attitudes toward handicapped persons are filled with misunderstanding and prejudice. For example, it is often assumed that anyone with a handicap does not, or should not, have sexual feelings and needs. Yet all human beings, even those with severe physical problems, are sexual beings as well.

When you are not used to being around someone who is blind or deaf, it is natural to feel somewhat awkward and uncomfortable. It is difficult to know exactly how to communicate. Blind or deaf young people often feel very isolated and frustrated because others may be hesitant to enter into relationships with them. Early ventures into love and sex are difficult enough, and facing others' discomfort because of a handicap only magnifies fears and self doubts. Sex education must sometimes be different for blind and deaf teenagers too. The blind may need to use three-dimensional models of sex organs and other body parts to really understand anatomy. The deaf may need to practice appropriate ways of communicating that will be understandable and non-threatening to others.

People with cerebral palsy or injury to their spinal cords may have difficulty controlling their muscular movements or may be partially paralyzed. Nevertheless, they still may desire sexual activity, and there are always ways of arranging suitable positions and special accommodations for most forms of sex to take place. Even individuals who are paralyzed in the region of their sex organs can participate in sex. Men often are still capable of erection and even ejaculation, while women may still achieve vaginal lubrication, with direct stimulation of the sex organs. The extent to which the sex organs still respond during sexual stimulation depends on the nature and extent of a spinal cord injury or disease. Many people who have become paralyzed report having learned a lesson that most of us could pay more attention to: that sex can be, and should be, far more than what our penises and vaginas can do.

Mentally retarded young people may not be seen as sexual people either, even though they also have sexual needs and feelings. It is particularly important for them to be given patient attention and sex education that is done in ways they can comprehend, so that they will learn how to manage their sexual feelings and behaviors in socially acceptable ways. They must also learn how to protect themselves from being sexually exploited by others.

The message from handicapped young people is clear: See us as people with the same hopes, fears, interests, and problems as everyone else. Give us a chance. Recognize us as sexual human beings who need love, closeness, and touching just like you.

### Sexual Exploitation

Exploitation refers to taking advantage of other people or "using" them. There is plenty of exploitation in many forms of irresponsible sex. Anytime that an individual is persuaded to become involved in sex through trickery or deceit, exploitation is going on. If one partner is interested primarily in selfish physical pleasure, but pretends that sex is a loving and spiritual thing, exploitation is going on. There are other forms of exploitation:

1. *Adults and Children.* One form of exploitation occurs when an adult persuades a child into some sort of sexual encounter. Some adults are particularly sexually attracted to youngsters and will attempt to take advantage of them. There are laws which prohibit these activities, and society and the courts often deal severely with offenders. It is true that children in some cases may seem not to object to the sexual advances of an adult, but courts usually place the burden of responsibility on the adult. Young people can be confused about sexual feelings, making them even more vulnerable to such adult exploitation. It is important for children to learn that their bodies are their own, and that grown ups do not have the right to intrude on their private body parts.

Evidence seems to indicate that most children are somewhat frightened and upset by such experiences, but there may be no permanent emotional harm. If parents of the child or others become overly upset about the incident in the child's presence, there may be more negative feelings created in the child. There is no evidence that the sex of the adult with whom a child has sexual contact affects in any way the young person's developing sexual preferences.

2. *Incest.* Sometimes sexual exploitation of children by adults takes place between members of the same family. The term *incest* usually refers to heterosexual intercourse between persons who are closely related (brother-sister; father-daughter; mother-son), but sexual activity may also occur between close relatives of the same sex. There are laws which prohibit incest, and our society is unaccepting of such behavior. Statistics indicate that incest is not common, but most professionals believe it to be more common than the figures suggest. Some young people suffer much anxiety and guilt about sexual activity with a relative, or sexual feelings for a family member, and may benefit from talking with a good counselor about their feelings. There are always people available who will be willing to help.

3. *Rape.* Another form of sexual exploitation is *rape.* This refers to a person being forced to participate in sexual activities without his or her willingness and consent, often through physical force or threats. The victim is most often a woman, forced into sexual activity by a man. This is a crime which girls and women find particularly frightening, since it represents the most violent form of sexual exploitation. There are courses and books which help to inform women about ways of preventing rape. Women's groups are encouraging rape victims to report the crime to authorities and to follow through to prosecution. In the past, laws made prosecution of rapists difficult. More recently, however, laws have made conviction of rapists more likely, and police officials and lawyers have become more aware of their own prejudices in dealing with these cases.

Being forced to have sex against one's will is a very frightening and dehumanizing experience. Rape victims must spend time dealing with a whole range of complicated emotions, and good counseling is usually a necessary part of that process. In most states, laws also exist which classify *any* sexual intercourse with a girl under a certain age (such as 17) as rape, even if she has consented to the intercourse. Since this is a legal definition, it is often called *statutory rape.*

4. *Exhibitionism and Voyeurism.* There are two other forms of sexual behavior which are exploitative, even though

there is no physical contact with the "victim." One is *exhibition-ism.* Exhibitionists are people, usually men, who obtain pleasure by exposing their sex organs to other people, usually strangers and usually women or children. Although exhibitionists do not physically harm others, some people may be insulted or offended by such behavior. The other exploitative behavior is *voyeurism,* refering to the enjoyment which some people get from seeing nude people or people engaged in sexual acts. The voyeur or "peeping Tom" is driven to peek in windows and violating others' privacy by the need for sexual pleasure. There are laws which can lead to the prosecution of exhibitionists and voyeurs.

Many people have mild feelings of exhibitionism. They simply enjoy having their bodies admired, including their sex organs. Many others have feelings of voyeurism. They enjoy seeing others in the nude. But the kinds of exhibitionism and voyeurism we've been discussing are examples of how sexual impulses can become exploitative when they are expressed without regard for the rights and choices of others.

### Sexually Transmitted Diseases

The sexually transmitted diseases (STD), formerly called venereal diseases (VD), are transmitted by direct sexual contact. Some are considered among the most serious diseases of the world and have reached epidemic proportions during recent years. (Figure 7.1) Any person who is sexually active or is thinking about having sexual activity should be familiar with the symptoms, prevention, and treatment of these diseases. Most forms of STD may be treated and cured with ease in the early stages, but putting off treatment can be dangerous!

The next few paragraphs will summarize some basic and important information on sexually transmitted diseases. More detailed information may be found in some of the books listed at the end of the chapter or at a library.

The germs which cause sexually transmitted diseases can survive only for a few seconds in the air, so the diseases are transmitted only by direct body contact. It is not possible to catch STDs from a toilet seat, dirty dishes, or clothing. You don't catch STDs from another person because he or she is dirty. You catch them because the other person caught them from

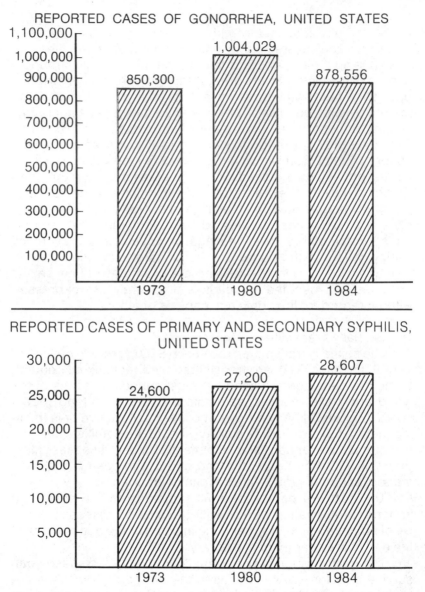

**Figure 7.1**  Reported cases of Gonorrhea and Syphilis, 1973–1984. (The actual number of cases is much higher than the figures shown here.)

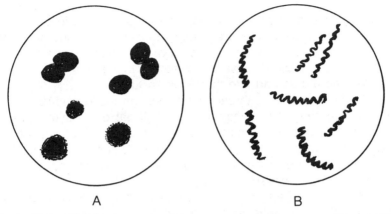

**Figure 7.2** (A) The bacteria which cause gonorrhea, magnified 1,500 times. (B) The spirochetes which cause syphilis, magnified 1,000 times.

another infected person. Like most other diseases, we really do not know where or when the sexually transmitted diseases started. They have been infecting human beings since the beginning of recorded history and probably long before. The infectious germs evolved along with other forms of life.

### STDs and their Symptoms

Any form of sexual contact in which the sex organs of one person are in direct contact with the sex organs, mouth, or anus of another can transmit the germs of gonorrhea or syphilis if they are present. Some of the symptoms of infection are as follows:

1. *Gonorrhea* ("Clap" or "The Drip") is caused by bacteria (Figure 7.2) that can attack the tissues lining the urethra, the cervix of women, the anus, the throat, or the eyelids.

In the penis, the symptoms usually begin to develop within a week after sexual contact with the infected person. The first sign is usually a burning and itching feeling during urination, and eventually severe pain during urination. This is usually accompanied by drainage of thick pus out of the penis. If untreated, the germs spread into the upper glands of the male reproductive system, the testes, bladder, and even the kidney.

In the vagina, the symptoms of gonorrhea are often not as easily detected. Pain and discharge of pus may not appear until much later. In the majority of women, few symptoms are noticed until the disease has progressed into a serious infection. The most common symptoms are vaginal discharge of pus, irritation of the major and minor lips in the vulva, and frequent painful urination. Again, if the disease is untreated, the germs may spread through the uterus and into the fallopian tubes.

In the mouth and throat, gonorrhea germs do not seem to survive very long. There may be a sore throat or no symptoms at all. In the anus or rectum of either sex, symptoms of gonorrhea may go unnoticed. There may be some irritation and discharge, but generally the disease goes undetected in the rectum until the germs have spread through the body.

In both men and women, lack of proper medical treatment for gonorrhea can lead to dangerous complications and illness. One serious result can be sterility, the inability to have children. The germs may also enter the bloodstream, leading to arthritis and other joint infections. If a mother is infected with gonorrhea at the time she is giving birth to a child, the bacteria can infect the baby's eyes and cause blindness. As a precaution against this, medications are always put in newborn babies' eyes which prevent infection.

2. *Syphilis* is caused by a germ known as a spirochete, a microscopic spiral-shaped organism (Figure 7.2). The germ is transferred from the infected person through the skin of the sexual partner. Once inside the body, the syphilis germs rapidly multiply. The disease, when untreated, has three stages:

a. *Early syphilis.* Within a month or two after contact with the infected person, a small, reddish, oozing sore appears on the skin. This is called a *chancre.* When it appears on the penis it is easily noticed. In the vagina or anus, however, the chancre is usually internal and often is not discovered. The chancre may also appear on or inside the mouth or elsewhere on the body. Syphilis is particularly contagious at this stage, since the chancre is filled with the spirochetes. Even without treatment, the chancre heals in 4 to 10 weeks. The germs have moved dangerously into the body.

b. *Secondary syphilis* may not become evident for several weeks. It is usually characterized by a rash over large portions of the body, along with a slight fever and general "run-

down" feeling. Sometimes there is a loss of hair from the scalp. Again, these symptoms gradually disappear as the germs begin to move deeper into body organs.
  c. *Late syphilis.* If medical treatment has not been given, the syphilis germs may gradually infect any portion of the body with serious results. The damage may not be recognized for many years after the infection first started. Among the more common problems of late syphilis are bone degeneration, heart and blood vessel disease, and brain infection which may lead to insanity. Untreated syphilis may eventually result in death.
  There are blood tests that show the presence of syphilis in its latter two stages. Some states require a blood test for syphilis before issuing a marriage license to a couple. If a pregnant woman has syphilis, the germs may be transmitted to the developing fetus, causing serious malformations and birth defects.
  3. *Chlamydia* is a microorganism only recently identified as causing a widespread and potentially serious sexually transmitted disease. It is believed that there are millions of new chlamydial infections each year. Part of the danger with chlamydia is that there are often no clearly identified symptoms until serious complications have developed. It is estimated that 70% or more of infected women and 10% of infected men do not develop symptoms in the earlier stages. The early symptoms, if they do develop, are similar to those of gonorrhea. They include burning and itching in the urethra and genital area, and sometimes discharge of pus. If untreated, more painful internal infections can develop that can cause permanent damage to the reproductive organs. If a chlamydial infection exists during pregnancy, the baby may be damaged and death of the unborn baby, or occasionally of the mother, can occur. Physicians have available quick, painless, and accurate tests to diagnose this disease that is now reaching epidemic proportions.
  4. *AIDS* stands for *Acquired Immune Deficiency Syndrome.* It is a disease that damages the body's natural immune system, reducing its ability to fight off diseases and infections. Consequently, AIDS victims are prone to developing rare forms of cancer, pneumonia, and other diseases that become life-

threatening. The symptoms of AIDS are highly variable, and usually involve the development of continual and persistent infections, while the general health of the individual gradually deteriorates. Researchers have discovered that a virus known as HTLV-III is associated with AIDS, and is believed to be either the cause or a contributing factor in this dangerous condition. Most current information suggests that the typical ways in which AIDS is spread are through shared needles for injection of drugs or through intimate sexual contact. Homosexual men who have had a large number of sexual partners seem to be at especially high risk of contracting the disease, although it is becoming an increasing problem for heterosexual men and women as well.

5. *Herpes* has now become one of the more common and more serious of the sexually transmitted diseases. Its name comes from the herpes virus that causes the infection, a germ very similar to the one which causes cold sores around the mouth. Usually within three weeks after sexual contact with an infected person, an area on the sex organs begins to itch or burn. Then, small, red blisters develop that become painful and ulcerated. The disease is most contagious in its blister form. In women, the blister may be internal, and therefore go unnoticed.

Like cold sores, genital herpes blisters eventually heal. However, the virus remains in the body, and there may be continuing, unpredictable flare-ups of the blisters. Since the virus is never actually eliminated from the body once contracted, there is no real "cure" for the disease. Some people never have any further outbreaks of the blisters after the initial infection. There are creams that may be applied to the blisters which appear to reduce discomfort.

There are two potential dangers for women with herpes infections. Medical researchers suspect that the virus may be one cause of cervical (in the cervix of the uterus) cancer. In addition, the virus can infect babies during the birth process, leading to serious disease or death of the infant. For this reason, caesarean delivery (see Chapter Ten) is often recommended for pregnant women who are known to have an active herpes infection.

6. *Venereal warts,* characterized by wart growths in or on the sex organs, are also caused by a virus. They are uncomfort-

able, and often painful. Medical treatment is important and usually involves surgical removal of the warts.

7. *Hepatitis B* is a viral liver infection often spread by sexual contact. There are many other forms of hepatitis that are not sexually transmitted, but hepatitis B is most typically spread through sex. It is especially common among homosexual males who participate in anal intercourse (see Chapter Five). The infection is characterized by fever, chills, nausea and a generally sick feeling that may persist for weeks. Although liver infections can sometimes be fatal, hepatitis B usually clears up on its own eventually. A new vaccine to prevent the disease is currently being tested, and may become the first vaccine to prevent an STD.

8. *Pubic lice* or *crabs* are tiny blood-sucking insects that become parasitic on the body. They most commonly infect the pubic hair area, causing troublesome itching. Other body hair regions may become infected, however. Although they are usually transmitted by direct body contact, this is one STD that may also be picked up through contact with contaminated bedding, clothes, towels, or toilet seats. Ordinary soap will not destroy pubic lice, but there are several prescribed medicated creams that will take care of them rapidly. Sheets, clothing, and other potentially contaminated materials must also be washed to prevent re-infection.

9. *Urethritis* refers to any infection of the urethra, and it may be caused by a variety of bacteria and yeasts that are spread through sexual contact. Urethritis usually causes itching and burning that may be particularly evident during or after urination. The symptons may be quite mild or severe, and such infections can be transmitted during sexual activity. One of the common causes of urethritis is chlamydia.

10. *Other Diseases Associated with Sex Organs.* There are three other sexually transmitted diseases that are less common in North America, but that can be very dangerous. They are chancroid, lymphogranuloma venereum (LGV), and granuloma inguinale. There are also many types of infections and inflammations that may affect the sex organs, although they are not all associated with sexual contact. Any discomfort, sores, warts, or

inflammations of the genitals should be discussed with a physician or STD clinic staff member regardless of their cause.

### Treatment and Prevention of STDs

Gonorrhea, syphilis, and chlamydia are easily treated by a physician. Both may be cured by a large enough injection of penicillin or other antibiotic. Taking penicillin pills alone will not cure the diseases and may be dangerous without a doctor's supervision. Pubic lice and most forms of urethritis also respond well to medical treatment. Since they are caused by viruses, AIDS, herpes, venereal warts, and hepatitis B are not curable by any medicine, but their uncomfortable symptoms may be relieved by appropriate treatment. A great deal of research is focusing on the development of vaccines to prevent AIDS and medications to cure this dread disease. At the present time, however, there is no cure for AIDS. Anyone who suspects the presence of a sexually transmitted disease should seek medical attention immediately! Simple tests can show whether or not the diseases are present, and—if so—appropriate treatment can be given. Many locations have clinics to treat STD, sometimes without charge. Public health agencies, telephone crisis centers, and counselors can often provide addresses of clinics and other health services.

There is an organization which provides a national, toll-free telephone hot line to offer information about sexually transmitted diseases. If you have any questions, or want to know the location of the nearest STD treatment clinic, the free telephone number of the VD National Hotline is 1-800-227-8922 (in California, 1-800-982-5883). No one will ask your name, and calls are completely confidential.

Sexually transmitted diseases may also be prevented. Preventive measures are a part of responsible sexual behavior. Some possibilities follow:

1. *Being selective and careful about sexual partners.* Casual, promiscuous sex with many different partners greatly increases the likelihood of contracting STD.

2. *Using a condom.* The condom ("rubber" or "bag") is worn on the penis. It may be purchased in any drug store and provides excellent protection for both partners when

properly used. Use of the condom and its value as a birth control device are discussed in Chapter Ten.

3. *Washing with soap and water* carefully before and after sexual activity can reduce the risk but is no guarantee of STD prevention. Urination following sex has also been recommended.

4. *Seeking treatment* of STDs immediately is essential so that they will not be spread.

5. *Informing partners* that you may have infected them with an STD or that you may have contracted STD from them is also a part of responsible sex. It may be difficult and embarrassing, but you owe it to them so they may seek treatment and prevent further spread of the disease. Some health agencies will ask your contacts, but rarely are all of these people followed up. If you find out you have any sexually transmitted disease, informing endangered contacts is *your* responsibility.

**When Sex Doesn't Work**

Sometimes our sex organs do not function quite the way we want or expect them to. Occasionally, that may be due to a lack of sexual excitement, so that the body does not begin its sexual response cycle (see p. 42). Other times, we may feel sexually aroused and be interested in reaching orgasm, but our bodies simply do not respond as expected.

Most people discover that their sex organs do not respond as they want from time to time. This is normal and may be expected occasionally. Individuals should try to accept such occasional problems without undue worry, criticism, or embarrassment—in themselves and in their sexual partners. In fact, worrying about them sometimes only increases the frequency of problems. If a person's sex organs *consistently* do not function as he or she wants—and the person is not being misled by exaggerated expectations from movies or novels—then it may be advisable to seek professional advice from a qualified sex therapist. Here are some of the difficulties that men and women may face, sometimes called sexual dysfunctions:

At some point in their lives, most men have a sexual experience in which they cannot get an erection of the penis or cannot keep the erection long enough to have orgasm. This is some-times called *impotence.* Fatigue, depression, and consumption of alcohol may lead to temporary erection difficulties. Some men are troubled by impotence for long periods of time. This problem is almost always caused by psychological factors, although physical conditions may be involved. It often goes away by itself, especially with an understanding and loving sexual partner, or—if serious enough—may be helped by sex therapy.

Men may also be concerned about reaching orgasm too rapidly—sometimes within a few seconds after intense sexual activity has begun. This is called *lack of ejaculatory control* or *premature ejaculation*, and is sometimes unsatisfying not only for the man but for his partner. This often occurs in young men who are highly excited during their first sexual experiences and also in men who have *learned* to reach orgasm rapidly during masturbation. They may also be helped to re-learn techniques for delaying their ejaculation and for making sex more enjoyable for their partners. Learning how to slow down during masturba-tion is one technique used. Another difficulty is *delayed ejacu-lation,* in which the man finds it difficult or impossible to reach orgasm, even though he has no problems maintaining an erec-tion. This can be very frustrating and may require professional advice.

Some women and men find it difficult to become sexually aroused and are generally uninterested in sexual contact. This may be a sign that they simply do not want sex at that time and need to feel that such a decision is all right. It may also signal deeper problems in need of professional attention. Some women also become sexually aroused, but have *difficulty reaching or-gasm.* It should be understood, however, that interest in sex varies with different individuals, and in our culture many women and men are not especially interested in reaching orgasm each time they have sex. For anyone concerned about lack of interest in sex or trouble reaching orgasm, sex therapy can often help.

A few women experience a problem called *vaginismus*, in which the vaginal muscles tighten so that sexual intercourse, or other forms of sexual activity in which vaginal penetration is made, can become painful or even impossible. (As mentioned in an ear-lier chapter, the male penis does *not* ever become "caught" in the vagina, however.) This dysfunction is also caused by psychological stress and may be helped by appropriate therapy.

Many of the problems discussed in this section are caused by anxiety about sex and the fear of not living up to one's own or a partner's expectations. They may also be caused by tensions and pressures that are not related to sex at all, but to stresses and misunderstandings in other areas of a relationship. In any case, these problems may be helped or prevented by working for healthy, guilt-free, relaxed relationships between loving, responsible individuals who care about one another's feelings—relationships in which sex is only a part. When problems do arise, however, it may be desirable to work on what might be getting in the way of effective communication between the partners, rather than concentrating on the sexual area right away. When sexual dysfunctions persist, they may be helped by learning particular techniques that help people become more relaxed and comfortable with sex. This may require the services of a competent, professional sex therapist. Some of the organizations listed in Appendix II (p. 187), including the American Association of Sex Educators, Counselors, and Therapists, may be able to help. There are a number of sex therapy clinics at large medical centers in North America that can also give advice, counseling, and treatment, although the cost of such services may be too steep for many young people to afford.

### Preventing Problem Sex
Even though sex-related problems occur at some point in nearly everyone's life, there are some suggestions which may help prevent at least some problems. Suggestions have been given elsewhere in this book, but a summary follows:

1. *Willingness to be honest* with oneself and with potential sex partners. What are you really feeling, and what are you really looking for in sex? Is sex something you really want right now for your life, or for your relationship with someone you love?

2. *Becoming comfortable with your own sexuality.* Many problems arise out of dissatisfaction with one's own sexual preferences and behaviors. To become comfortable with your sexuality, learn more about sex through books and courses, and spend some time thinking about what is sexually interesting and

uninteresting for you. Then ask yourself whether the things you are doing or not doing sexually are the result of your own choices. Have you been doing what you think you are "supposed" to do or what you think other people—including your sexual partner—"expect" of you? You may want to talk about sex with a good counselor.

3. *Good communication* with friends and people you love can prevent many sex problems. If you cannot talk openly about sex and your feelings with someone you love, or about such practical problems as hygiene or birth control, you are probably not ready for responsible sex with that person.

4. *Being Realistic about Sex.*   Don't try to model yourself or your sexuality after someone you have read about or have seen in movies or on television. Be yourself and find your own sexuality. Remember that sex is not always spectacular. Not placing unrealistic sexual expectations on yourself or your partner will allow you both the freedom to be yourselves sexually.

5. *Maintaining a Sense of Responsibility* toward self and others is also essential to prevention of sex problems. Responsible sex does not lead to unwanted pregnancy, spread of sexually transmitted diseases, or the hurting of oneself or others. Caring about life and people carries with it important responsibilities.

6. *Knowing When to Seek Help.*   As much as we like to feel independent and "in-control" of situations, some problems simply cannot be dealt with alone. Sometimes if we neglect to get proper outside help, the problem simply grows and becomes

even more troublesome or dangerous. Knowing when and how to seek appropriate help can prevent most problems from getting worse.

### Problem Sex and Your Life

The following exercises can move you toward a better understanding of your values concerning certain sexual problems and encourage you to think about the avenues for help which you know about.

1. *What would you suggest?*

Consider each of the following sex-related problems. If a good friend brought the problem to you, what suggestions would you have for your friend? Keep in mind that you are not expected to help resolve the problem all by yourself, but only to suggest some ways in which the friend could find help.

In a classroom setting, each of these situations can be role-played aloud, with other members of the class commenting on the results and making further suggestions.

a. A boy confides to you that he is worried about a burning feeling when he urinates. Two weeks before, he had sexual intercourse with a girl who is also a friend of yours. It was his first sexual experience and he feels guilty about it.

b. A girl tells you that the night before, a boy whom she was dating for the first time physically forced her to have sexual intercourse. She has been too frightened and embarrassed to tell anyone else about the experience. She is afraid that she might now be pregnant.

c. You learn that a boy who is a neighbor and close friend of yours recently persuaded a five-year-old girl to remove all of her clothes in his garage. They were discovered by the girl's father, who called the police. The boy was given a warning by the police, but not arrested. Everyone in your neighborhood is talking about the incident, and the boy is too ashamed to come out of his house.

d. A girl telephones and hesitantly tells you that a boy with whom she recently had sexual intercourse just told her that he has syphilis. She is upset and frightened and asks for your advice.

e.   A boy tells you that another boy in the class has suggested to him that they have homosexual sex. He is very
frightened of and opposed to homosexuality, and he feels
very angry and insulted, as if his manhood has been chal-
lenged. He is planning some way to hurt the boy who made
the suggestion to him.

f.   A girl tells you that she thinks she is in love with another
girl, her best friend. She thinks the other girl may feel the
same way, but she is frightened to talk with her about it.
If her friend is disgusted, and she is rejected, she knows she
will never be able to stand it. If her friend does feel the same
way, she might not be able to handle it either, since she
herself is very nervous about the idea of being "homosexual."

2.   *Your worries*

a.   After thoroughly reading this chapter, read through the
following list and note which of the items you have been concerned or upset about—either as a part of your own life or the
life of someone close to you. Also, pick the one or two which
have been the biggest problem(s) for you:

| | |
|---|---|
| masturbation | incest |
| homosexual feelings | rape |
| sexual fantasies and dreams | exhibitionism |
| the size or shape of your | voyeurism |
|     sex organs | sexually transmitted dis- |
| the size or development of |     ease |
|     your body | erection difficulty |
| "how far to go" sexually | lack of ejaculatory control |
| guilt about sex | inability to have an orgasm |
| fear of pregnancy | vaginismus |
| lack of interest in sex | inability to become sex- |
| |     ually aroused |

b.   Now consider those items which you have considered
to be sex-related problems for your life. How did you handle the
problems? If the problem is still with you, are you doing anything
about it? Should you be seeking some sort of outside help to
deal with the problem? If you feel the need to work on a sexual
problem, why not *design a plan of action right now?* Here are
some questions to think about which may help in thinking through
your design:

— Do you have adequate information about your problem? (See references listed at the end of the chapter.)

— Do you know if other people—including professional counselors—would consider your "problem" to be truly a problem?

— Is the problem one which requires medical help, and, if so, where can you find a physician, nurse, or other medical professional whom you trust and can talk to?

— Should you talk about the problem with a counselor? (See Chapter Six.)

— Do you sometimes think that you are the only person who has this problem? You can be sure that many others share the same problem.

3. *More information*

This chapter discusses sex problems very briefly. As a project for school, or simply for your own information, you might do some more reading on the following topics. Some of the books listed at the end of the chapter can provide more information:

Incest relationships

Rape and how the law deals with rapists and their victims

Exhibitionism and Voyeurism

Laws concerning sexual behavior

Changing social values concerning homosexuality and bisexuality

Syphilis and gonorrhea

The "other" venereal diseases

Herpes or chlamydia as an increasing problem

The "other" sexually transmitted diseases

The sexual dysfunctions and how they are treated

## For Further Reading

Gordon, Sol. *Facts About STD.* Fayetteville, NY (P.O. Box 583): Ed-U-Press, 1983.

Gordon, Sol; Weening, Charles; Kratoville, Betty; and Biklen, Doug. *Living Fully: A Guide for Young People with a Handicap, Their Parents, Their Teachers, and Professionals.* Fayetteville, NY (P.O. Box 583): Ed-U-Press, 1975.

Kelly, Gary F. *Sexuality: The Human Perspective.* Woodbury, NY: Barron's Educational Series, 1980.

Lumiere, Richard and Cook, Stephani. *Healthy Sex and Keeping it that Way.* New York: Simon and Schuster, 1983.

Mintz, T. and Mintz, L.M. *Threshold: Straightforward Answers to Teenagers' Questions About Sex.* New York: Walker, 1978.

Morris, Jan. *Conundrum.* New York: Signet Books, 1974. (A transsexual describes the long transition from being a man to becoming a woman.)

Neumann, Hans and Simmons, Sylvia. *Dr. Neumann's Guide to the New Sexually Transmitted Diseases.* Washington: Acropolis Books, 1983.

# 8  Loving and Being Together As Sexual People

Although sexual feelings may be experienced, enjoyed, and even savored by oneself, full expression of our sexuality usually involves other people. It seems that to delight fully in what our sexual responses have to offer, there needs to be a sharing of those responses with another. Since our sexual feelings are such a deeply personal aspect of our selves, it is quite understandable that we might want to share them with a person for whom we have a deep affection—a person with whom we share love.

In this chapter, we will take a look at love and intimacy and at how they relate to our lives as sexual people. This is a tall order, for there are a number of fine books on these subjects, and for centuries authors and poets have dealt with the myriad intricacies and complexities of love. It is a confusing subject, and most of us experience some very real confusion and hurt as we try to deal with loving feelings at various times in our lives. I have talked with hundreds of people—young, old, and in between—who were attempting to understand loving relationships in their lives. Often, the part that sex plays in those relationships is a major concern.

### What is Love?

It seems that the word "love" has become a catchall term in our language. I understand that the Eskimos have fifteen different words to describe different types of the substance we call simply *snow.* Surely we could use that many different words to do justice to the many aspects of love which we experience. I talk of loving my parents and my brother; I love my wife and my dog; I often say that I love a certain book, or a movie, or a piece of music. We hear about loving God and of loving humankind. Many people use the term "making love" to refer to having sexual intercourse. Surely these forms of love differ in at least some respects.

Psychologist Erich Fromm, in his famous book *The Art of Loving,* maintains that love is indeed an *art.* By this, he means that it is not enough just to sit back and wait to get lucky and "fall in love." Instead, we must spend time *learning* what love is and what it means to our lives. It is essential that we put real *effort* into loving others; love is something which must be worked at! In other words, to be successful with love, we must actively practice it as an art worthy of our careful attention.

We live in a society where love and sex are important topics. That is easy to notice when we examine the themes of books, films, music, magazine stories, television plays, and even advertising. Love is everywhere! It is also portrayed much of the time in very unrealistic ways; it is often made to seem simple and uncomplicated—once the love conflict in the story line is resolved, the couple lives happily ever after without having to *work* at love again. As most of us can testify, love is usually entered into with great hopes and expectations and promises, yet hardly any human venture ends in failure as often as does love. Perhaps some of what follows in this chapter will make the picture clearer.

### Falling in Love and Being in Love

Think for a moment about all of the people you have seen in the past week, or in your lifetime. How many of them could you say you know? How many could be called "friend"? Probably not very many of them. It is part of the human condition that most of us are strangers to one another. We are separate; we are isolated. In some ways, we are alone. Some of us feel that separateness more acutely than others, but for most of us there is an inner longing to be closer to others. That longing may be shown through the desire to "belong" or "fit in" with a group of people our own age. It may be seen in the need to play a sport that has a team spirit. And with its greatest intensity, the longing may be felt at times as a deep need to become emotionally and physically closer to a particular person.

Whenever I have an encounter with another human being that involves the lowering of our barriers—allowing us to see each other more honestly and openly without the usual masks and hidden emotions—I feel marvelously happy and exhilarated. I am not as separate; my longing for closeness is, for a time, quieted. This is part of the process of *"falling* in love"—a relatively sudden and intense feeling of intimacy and closeness. It feels good, and sometimes the sexual attraction or sharing of sexual feelings which may become a part of such an encounter make it all feel even better.

However, we never "fall" forever. The falling in love process is not a lasting one. For awhile, the two people continue to break through more and more barriers, getting closer and closer. But eventually the process becomes less exciting and interesting. Even sexual involvement may gradually lose some of its luster. If the individuals have not moved more toward a lasting state of *"being* in love," their mutual boredom and disappointment will end the falling process, and there will be little left to keep them together.

So now, what is this "being in love" all about? Each of us must discover what this real loving is going to be for his or her own life. I am working on it in my life and will be for a very long time to come. Yet, by talking about love with a wide variety of people—alone and in couples—I have come to believe that there are certain elements that seem to be common to any relationship where people are *working* at being in love.

### Qualities of Being in Love

*Choice.* We consciously choose what people we can let ourselves be fully close to, and we choose how much of ourselves we feel able to show to any other person. But the choice must be mutual if it is to be love. All individuals involved in the loving relationship must choose one another.

*Giving.* To love, we must give to another. This does not mean giving up or sacrificing, nor does it just mean giving objects or money. Instead, there is a mutual giving of qualities of one's life: experiences, feelings, humor, sadness, and all things which are a part of us. Giving brings us joy and it enriches us; it helps bring us closer.

*Closeness.* People in love strive for more honest knowledge of each other—knowledge of past life, of ideas and values, of feelings and hopes, of weaknesses and defects and disappointments, of what their bodies have to offer. To reach continuously new depths of intimacy requires *time, privacy,* and *trust.*

*Trust.* We come to trust another as we gradually risk revealing our inner thoughts and feelings to that other person. In love, if the other person treats what we reveal with care, gentleness, and respect, we learn to feel a sense of trust. Mutual trust seems to be essential to being in love.

*Caring.* Being in love also means being actively concerned for the person whom we love: concerned for that individual's feelings and needs. People who love care about seeing each other grow and be happy and fulfilled.

*Responsibility.* When we choose to be close to another individual and care about him or her, then we have accepted a degree of responsibility to respond to that other person's needs—whether they are expressed or not. I do not mean that this is in any way a duty. Instead it is a *willingness* to be responsive to another human being.

*Respect.* This is a quality that is often misunderstood. When I respect others, it does not mean that I do what they want because I am afraid of them. It means that I see them as the unique individuals they are. It means that I will want to see the other person emerge as he or she is, as fully as possible.

*Delight.* Loving involves mutual delight as we care for one another and share and watch one another emerge. When we allow another person to grow or give him or her pleasure, then we delight in ourselves and in each other.

*Self-awareness.* It seems that the more we know about ourselves, the more we can understand what is happening between us and others. Being in love necessitates a continuing struggle to keep in touch with what is happening inside ourselves. In that way, what we give to one another is clearer and more meaningful.

Those are at least some of the qualities people in love find to be important if the relationship is to be a lasting one. There are many other words that could be used, and you may have other qualities you would want to add to the list. Feel free to do so. You may also feel that I am pointing toward some sort of perfection that is not very plausible for most people. Maybe, but I have seen a great many people make remarkable progress in establishing good loving relationships. Of course, we all have to struggle with these qualities, but I believe that struggle is part of what love is all about.

Perhaps the most important point of all is that to achieve any measure of success with these qualities, *work* is required. By work I mean being consciously aware of what you are trying to accomplish, concentrating on your goals, and having as much patience as you can muster because it won't be quick or easy. I also mean working at these qualities even when it is a little difficult, even though you may not be quite "in the mood."

More and more, then, I have been realizing in my own life that I just cannot sit back and wait for "love" to fall in my lap. I am going to have to try consciously to make my relationships with other persons good for us—to make them loving. And I am also realizing that it is very worth the effort.

### Whom Do We Love?

It seems, then, that loving another person involves the *total relationship* you share with that person, along with the relationships you share with others. At this point, it is important that we take a look at the different types of love, each based on the type of person or object that is being loved. Let us consider briefly six kinds of love which seem to be a part of human experience:

1. *Love for humankind.* This is the kind of love for others we feel as we realize that all of us have a great deal in

common. When we really feel our oneness and equality with our fellow humans, we can begin to care about them.

2. *Love of God.* In most religions, this goes hand-in-hand with loving our fellow humans. It is often emphasized in religions that love of God is shown by a feeling of oneness with a divine being which is expressed in the actions the person takes.

3. *Love for someone we can help.* It is this sort of love which a mother and father feel for their child or that you might feel for a younger brother or sister.

4. *Love of parents* is an example of the kind of love we feel toward someone who has protected us and taken care of us when we needed help.

5. *Love for oneself* is often misunderstood and confused with conceit. It does not refer to the sort of thing I once saw in a student of mine. He was always saying, "I am great!" Instead, it means having self-respect and being able to trust in your own actions; it means caring about what happens to you as well as others around you. Many psychologists believe that before you can be a truly complete person and before you can really work at loving others, you must first care for yourself.

6. *Love with sexual longing.* This is the kind of love that involves the desire to share sexually with another person—to feel the closeness and excitement a sexual union can achieve. It is more than the pleasure of bodies physically being together, but includes all of the emotional aspects of people deepening their levels of communication and mutual delight.

### Where Does Sex Fit?

Now we need to take a look at how sex fits—or doesn't fit—into this picture. One of the perennial questions has been: Can sex have real meaning without love? Of course it can. There are a great many ways in which people enjoy the excitement of their own sexual feelings and the sharing of those feelings with others without many aspects of love being present at all.

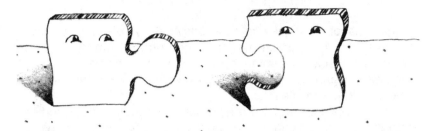

For example, almost all boys and the majority of girls begin to get in touch with their sexual feelings and the enjoyment they can yield through masturbation. This refers to stimulating the sexual organs with the hands or in some other way to produce sexual stimulation and the pleasure of sexual climax or orgasm (also see Chapter Three). Masturbation, along with the fantasies that may accompany it in the mind, may be intensely pleasurable and exciting ways of expressing our sexuality, and yet love has little to do with it.

Likewise, some people have always enjoyed casual sexual encounters with others. Without any emotional involvement or loving feelings expected, some agree to share sex with one another and enjoy that sharing to the fullest. Others sometimes find it difficult to become sexually involved in such a casual way without feeling some sense of guilt. Still others would not even consider having quick sex with another. This is one of those areas you may want to spend some time thinking about in order to decide what your feelings and values are.

In this chapter, we certainly should not lose sight of the fact that for many people who are working at the sharing of a loving relationship, sex is an important part of the sharing. People "in love" consistently report that a good sexual encounter often deepens their sense of communication with one another and indeed strengthens their love.

If you read back over the "Qualities of Being in Love" which were listed a few pages back, you may readily see how sex might fit into each of those qualities. People who share sexually in positive ways *choose* to do so with each other. The coming together of our bodies in sex certainly represents a *giving* of oneself and an unparalleled *closeness* and *delight* with another person. When we are together sexually with another human being, certainly the dimensions of *trust, caring, responsibility,* and *respect* in our dealings with that person may be of the utmost importance. And as we share sex with someone else, we also increase our own *self-awareness;* we get closer to our own bodies and feelings and what they have to offer us.

But it certainly would be a mistake to assume that good sex is all there is to a good loving relationship. Likewise, it would be naive to believe that sexual contact with another person can only be fully enjoyable and successful when loving feelings are involved. Each of us—as the individuals we are and want to be—must decide what the level of interaction between love and sex will be in his or her life. There are no fast and ready rules which seem to apply successfully to everyone.

### Some Value Questions

As a way of helping you begin to think more fully about how sex and love will fit together for you, consider the following questions. Remember, there are no "right" and "wrong" answers—just *your* answers. And do not expect to find your answers in the next few minutes; they may be months or even years away.

1.  Would you have sex with a person whom you have just met at a party and find physically attractive?
2.  How do you feel about people who assure others that they love them, just so that they will have sex with them?
3.  Would you consider paying another person to have sex with you? Would you consider being paid to have sex?
4.  What kinds of qualities and feelings do you want to have in a relationship before you are ready to have a sexual contact with the other person?

5. What kind of loving relationships have you experienced in your life? How did sex become involved in those relationships? As you look back, how do you feel about the relationships?
6. Right now in your life, are there one or more people with whom you would be interested in sharing a sexual encounter? What kinds of relationships do you have with this person (or these people)? If the opportunity for sex comes along, what do you think you will do?
7. Do you or could you love a member of your own sex? If so, how is this different from or the same as the love you might feel for a member of the opposite sex?
8. What have your parents, school, and religious group taught you about the relationship of sex and love? How important to you are these teachings?

**For Further Reading**

Bohannan, Paul. *Love, Sex, and Being Human.* New York: Doubleday, 1969.

Booker, Diana. *Love.* New York: Julian Messner, Simon & Schuster, 1985.

Fromm, Erich. *The Art of Loving.* New York: Bantam Books, 1970.

Gussin, Gilda; Buxbaum, Ann; and Danforth, Nicholas. *Self Discovery, Caring, Loving and Sexuality.* Boston: Management Sciences for Health, 1984.

Hamilton, Eleanor. *Sex with Love: A Guide for Young People.* Beacon Press, 1978.

Johnson, Eric. *Love and Sex in Plain Language.* New York: Harper and Row, 1985.

Johnson, Eric. *People, Love, Sex, and Families.* New York: Walker and Co., 1985.

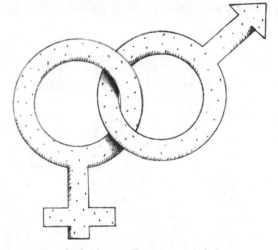

# 9    Marriage and Other Partnerships

In recent years, attitudes toward marriage have been changing. I have heard many young people make statements such as: "I'll never get married!" "Marriage is just legalized sex." "Why get married when you can just live together!" "Marriage is out of date." In this chapter, we shall take a closer look at marriage in today's society and how sex fits into that picture. We shall also briefly examine other close partnerships between people that do not involve marriage.

The soaring rates of separation and divorce have been frightening some people. There was a 34% increase in the divorce rate during the 1960s and an 80% increase during the decade of the seventies. At the present time, about 40% of marriages now taking place end in divorce.

Of course, it is also important to note that recent changes in laws have made divorce much easier from a legal standpoint. The divorce statistics may not mean that the rate of unhappy, unsuccessful marriages has increased. Such marriages may simply now be easier to get out of, or more couples may be deciding that when communication stops—when love and caring, warmth and pride, cannot be sustained in a relationship—it is time to call it quits. In any case, plenty of marriages are not working. As this chapter points out, it is a step to be taken with care and planning.

### Changing Patterns of Marriage

During past centuries, marriage among the wealthy classes was often a convenient business arrangement. Fathers made arrangements with prospective husbands for their daughters to give them a certain amount of property and money upon marriage. Often, the young people knew one another only slightly and certainly did not have a loving relationship. One important result of these marriages was children. The children made families even more powerful, as they carried on combined traditions and took their share of property and money.

Among the poorer, working classes a man would often seek a wife as a cook, housekeeper, and convenient partner for sex, again with little "love" between them. The children of these marriages were often considered status symbols—beings for a father (and to a lesser degree, a mother) to be proud of. The husband worked to provide money and shelter, while the wife fulfilled her duties in the home.

In some cultures today, marriages that are arranged by parents for convenience and property are still common. In nearly all of these cultures, it is the sons who share in the property of their fathers, while arrangements are made for daughters to marry, taking to their husbands smaller portions of their fathers' money or property.

Over the past 150 years, the predominant patterns of marriage have changed in most aspects of our society. One of the most significant changes has been the emphasis on marrying because of love for and commitment to another person. Gradually, it became important for a man and woman to spend time getting to know one another, while their love grew and became stronger. Eventually the two might decide that they wanted to be married so that they could live together, share property, share sex, and raise a family. Marriage was the bond by which the government approved such a relationship and established certain legal responsibilities and limits for the two people. Usually, marriage included a religious ceremony in which the two people promised to uphold their religious customs and traditions as well.

Today, there are many differing points of view on what marriage should and should not be. Some people still hold the view of marriage described in the last paragraph, while others find that view overly sentimental and unrealistic. We shall now explore some modern views of marriage.

### New Outlooks on Marriage

So why do people get married anyway? The answers to that question aren't as simple as they once were. Many feel that a good case can be made for *not* being married as well. Nevertheless, a great many people are still marrying, for a great variety of reasons. Some very good marriages seem to grow out of foundations such as the following:

1. *Deepened Commitment.* In the last chapter, we dealt with loving relationships and the amount of work involved in "being in love." Some couples who are working at love choose to formalize their commitment and establish a partnership as husband and wife. The marriage ceremony itself involves an exchange of vows between the partners—promises that two people make to one another. Today, it is very common for the two people to write their own vows—to decide what they are willing to promise. An important part of getting ready for marriage can be working out together what promises each individual is willing to make.

Some people believe that the legal ties of marriage make it more difficult for married persons to simply "cut out" on their partners during rough times, instead of sticking with it and working on problems. Hopefully, however, a good marriage is based on a mutual commitment to work on difficulties, rather than a legal obligation to do so.

2. *Raising a Family.* Although society is gradually becoming more accepting of unmarried couples who live together and share sexual feelings, it is still generally believed that children are better raised within a marriage. Many couples decide to marry when they want to have children and feel that marriage provides a more socially acceptable environment in which to raise them. Not everyone agrees that marriage should be necessary before raising a family. There is good evidence, too, that single parents can be very effective. Most professionals believe that there must be more in a good marriage than *just* the desire to have children.

There must be a real commitment between two individuals who want to share many other aspects of their lives. More about being a parent in Chapter Ten.

3. *Respect for Tradition.* Some people marry because they would not feel comfortable living together or having sexual intercourse without marriage. All of us must decide how important the values of our parents, religion, and society are to our own lives. Undoubtedly, some couples marry out of respect to parents or others, instead of living together without marrying. Such respect for tradition has its place, but no marriage is advisable until both partners have had a chance to understand what marriage means to them and to feel ready for it.

4. *Symbolizing Fulfillment and Security.* As loving relationships develop, the individuals involved find more and more fulfillment and security in one another. One reason why many people marry is that they want to make a formal statement, symbolizing their desire to continue sharing with each other the many changing aspects of their lives. Healthy marriages give both the man and woman room to grow. They can both be individuals, while sharing a relationship together.

5. *Practical Considerations.* In our society, people who are married are recognized as "next of kin," and this relationship gives them special benefits that unmarried couples do not have. They may file joint income tax returns, inherit each other's property, be included under employee health insurance plans, open joint bank accounts, and assume many other rights and privileges in relation to each other's lives.

### Homosexual Marriage

In some cases, a long-standing unmarried relationship between a man and a woman can achieve legal status as *common-law marriage.* In our culture, however, even a long-standing, loving, committed relationship between members of the same sex cannot be legalized. Some homosexual couples, who have desired religious sanction for their love or have wanted to symbolize their continuing commitment, have exchanged vows with each other in "holy union" ceremonies. These are performed by ministers of gay churches or other members of the clergy, but none of these unions has been legally recognized.

Homosexual couples resent being denied the practical benefits of legal marriage, but most gay-rights organizations are not
working very hard to change the marriage laws. Rather, they are
working for legal changes to ensure that all couples who have
formed committed relationships—whether they are of the same or
of the opposite sex—have the same rights and privileges as those
who have chosen to formalize their commitment in marriage.

### Not Being Married

Marriage simply isn't for everyone. Some people either do
not want or are not ready for either the formal or informal commitments, responsibilities, compromises, and problems that go
with marriage. It is also a fact that many individuals live fulfilling,
satisfying, happy lives without ever marrying.

Marriage during the teenage years is especially risky. Most
professionals try to persuade teenagers either not to get married
or to consider such a step with extreme caution. This is done with
good reason, since about half of teenage marriages end in divorce. When most of those divorced couples married as teenagers, they were happy and quite convinced that their marriages
would work. They were wrong. In the past, most people in the
United States were married by the age of twenty-two. Gradually,
that age is rising, and that may mean that the divorce rate will
eventually go down. Again, it is generally accepted that a better
time for most people to consider marriage is around the age of
twenty-five or older.

Some couples marry for the wrong reasons. Here are some
poor reasons, in themselves, for getting married.

1. *Sexual Attraction.* A marriage based on physical attraction alone will probably run into serious trouble eventually. A
relatively small amount of time in marriage is spent in actual
sexual contact. A physically attractive and sexually responsive
partner may be a very desirable husband or wife, but other qualities must also be taken into consideration.

2. *To gain Independence.* Some people marry so that
they can leave home and gain independence from their parents.
Good marriages are usually the result of two partners who bring
a certain type of independence to the marriage with them, and
not a need to "escape" from home.

3. *Search for Security.* There are many different kinds of security people expect from marriage. But if you marry just for financial security, or for a convenient sexual partner, or out of fear of losing the other person, it is likely you will be disappointed by your marriage.

4. *Pressure from Others.* Americans place a high premium on marriage, and nearly 95% of them marry at least once. Many unmarried young men and women in their early twenties begin to feel the pressure from family and society that say, "Isn't it about time you were thinking about marriage and settling down?" As we have already stated, most people may not be ready for marriage until later in their lives, and some are never ready. Marriage should never happen just because "it's the thing to do."

5. *Unwanted Pregnancy.* It is not unusual for a young couple to marry because they have started a pregnancy. If the pregnancy was not wanted, however, and one or both of the partners feels unprepared for the responsibilities of marriage and parenthood, the marriage is most likely a mistake. Creating an unhappy, unwilling marriage may not be the best or most responsible way to deal with a pregnancy.

6. *For Status.* Some people marry out of the belief that they will "fit in" socially better if they have a spouse (husband or wife). Sometimes a marriage partner is chosen because he or she is attractive and looks like the "perfect" husband or wife. Such a superficial reason for marriage can hardly lead to lasting happiness or lifetime fulfillment.

### Other Partnerships

Today, many individuals are deciding to pair up without marrying. Some couples are living together, sharing sex, sharing the practical necessities of life, and developing strong loving commitments, without commiting themselves to marriage. Some of these relationships do not survive for long; others have continued for many years; and still others eventually lead to marriage.

It is typical for people to think of sex when they think of marriage. A sixteen-year-old boy I know recently told me that he thought marriage is just "legalized sex," and that the only reason people marry is to have socially approved sexual intercourse. Currently, many people do *not* feel this to be true, and accept that sexual intercourse may be all right and meaningful in a loving, committed relationship, even without marriage.

At several points in this book, sex without marriage has been discussed. It has been stated repeatedly that each individual must make her or his own responsible decisions about sex, based on careful thought and an awareness of one's own values. This is also true of any kind of partnership where a man and woman live together without being married. There are some young people who share an apartment with someone of the opposite sex, but do *not* share sex. There are also groups of men and women who live together without sharing sex. Again, each individual in a partnership must make decisions, taking into consideration the values and feelings of other people who are significant to his or her life.

Most couples who are involved in unmarried partnerships do not want children. As stated earlier, children are best raised in a committed relationship which is expected to last, since they need that kind of consistency and security. That is not to say that unmarried or single parents cannot be good parents; it simply may be more difficult for them. Most unmarried heterosexual couples who share sex take the responsibility of using birth control methods, as discussed in the next chapter.

Parents react in many different ways when they learn that an unmarried son or daughter is "living with" someone of the opposite sex. I have seen the reaction in which parents are shocked and refuse to even speak to the son or daughter. Some parents decide that the relationship is acceptable but do not wish the couple to share the same bed when they come home for a visit. Other parents have no difficulty accepting the partnership and are even happy that the couple is sharing sex. Many young couples who have decided to "live together" have trouble deciding whether or not to tell their parents. Yet, they also find it difficult to predict their parents' reaction.

### Changing Sex Roles
Healthy relationships, whether married or unmarried, give both partners room to grow in directions of their own choosing.

It is important for both of them to be independent individuals while sharing a relationship together. In the traditional marriage, however, it was sometimes impossible for the partners to be who they really were as individuals, or to find out about the best that each of them had to offer each other. Instead, they were busy doing what was expected of them as men or women.

Traditionally, a man was a person who worked to earn money for his family and acted as protector and businessman for family affairs. A woman traditionally took more responsibility for household tasks and raising children. As we began to explore in Chapter Three, traditional male-female roles are changing, and that applies to marriages as well.

Current social trends are emphasizing the equality of women and men, and this influence is being felt in marriages. Many women find work outside the home enjoyable and fulfilling, and wish to contribute to the family financially. Likewise, men are taking over duties in the home, and are demonstrating patience and sensitivity in dealing with children. In other words, many married people are searching for the activities that feel right for them and that contribute to a happier marriage, without letting themselves be locked in unreasonable old patterns.

One of the traditional patterns was for the husband to be the one who initiated sex. In the past, it was mistakenly believed that men always had a stronger sex drive than women, and it was therefore the wife's duty to have sexual intercourse whenever her husband desired. We now know that women may indeed have as strong an interest in sex as men. It is accepted today that it is all right for women to desire sex and for wives to initiate sex with their husbands. No longer is the husband's sexual pleasure the most important goal. Both the man and woman have a right to enjoy sex and gain pleasure from it, and both have the right *not* to participate when they wish.

Some homosexual couples have attempted to adopt traditional "male" and "female" roles, but most gay men and women report that they have always felt themselves to be at an advantage in finding true equality in a relationship. They could not *automatically* adopt a role, but were forced to discover for themselves the qualities of love or caring, understanding or responsibility, that each of them could best bring to the relationship. This does not mean that homosexual couples have an easier job establishing the communication necessary to develop these qualities, but that they find it easier to know they must develop them.

## Working at a Relationship

While organizing this chapter, I asked several people what they thought teenagers should know about marriage and other committed relationships. One twenty-four-year-old woman who re-married after her first marriage ended in divorce, put it like this:

> Make sure they understand that a good marriage takes constant effort. Not just once in awhile, but day-in and day-out effort. It's not always fun, and it's certainly not always easy. But it's worth it.

Her thoughts were echoed by everyone else I talked to who had attempted a committed relationship with another person. The relationship and one's partner in it simply cannot be taken for granted. There must be a strong commitment to work at caring about each other and communicating with each other. That means being willing to take the other person's feelings, needs, and ideas into consideration along with your own. It also means working out the practical details of living together and taking care of cleaning, meals, and finances.

Two people are never exactly alike in their habits, interests, or goals for the future. In marriage, then, when two people live together and work toward a future together, there has to be *compromise.* That will mean that both partners must "give" a little, sometimes not doing things quite the way either of them alone might prefer. It may also mean that the two will sometimes get angry with one another. When that happens, good communication is really put to the test. If both can admit their feelings and deal with them as constructively as possible, then anger does not have to lead to destructive, hurting name-calling that accomplishes little.

## Partnerships and Successful Sex

Most couples want to develop a successful sexual relationship. First, I need to explain what I mean by "successful." It seems that a successful sexual relationship in a partnership includes the following qualities:

1. Both partners participate in choosing when to become involved sexually and do not feel manipulated or coerced into sex by the other.

2. Both partners generally find their sexual contacts to be pleasurable, satisfying, and desirable experiences.

3. Both partners usually feel satisfied that their bodies have functioned sexually as they wanted and that they are able to have orgasm, or sexual climax, when they wish.

4. There is some sense of freedom between the partners for variety and experimentation in their sexual activities, provided it is acceptable to both.

5. Neither partner feels pressured to participate in sexual activities which he or she does not find appealing or enjoyable.

6. Neither partner feels pressured to have sex when he or she does not wish or solely for the other partner's enjoyment.

When people live together, they are bound to have more opportunity for sex. Likewise, the longer the two are together, the greater the likelihood for sexual problems—or an unsatisfactory sexual relationship—to develop. Like any other aspect of a healthy, growing partnership, sex takes some effort too.

It is important to remember, however, that most sexual problems cannot be worked out apart from the basic problems in the overall relationship. Part of working on these problems is that *good communication* I keep emphasizing. If one partner is feeling used, dissatisfied, or unhappy about sex or any other aspect of the relationship, but does not share the feeling with the other, things will probably not improve. *Compromise* is necessary in sex too. It is seldom that both partners are exactly alike in their sexual needs and preferences. In other words, your partner may not be interested in sex at the same times you are or may not enjoy the same kinds of sexual activity as you. Therefore, there will have to be compromises in both directions to develop a successful sexual relationship. In the sexual area and all others, compromise does not have to mean that you give up your own values or your own sense of individuality and self-worth. Many people believe that no relationship is worth preserving when sacrifices of this sort are required to sustain it.

One of the important questions to be resolved in many relationships is whether or not both partners are satisfied to have sex only with one another. Traditional marriage has meant the need for fidelity—having sex only with one's husband or wife. When a married person has extramarital sexual intercourse—sex with someone other than the husband or wife—it is defined as *adultery*. Most states consider adultery illegal and most religions consider it immoral. Nevertheless, many people do have sex outside their partnerships. For some, this is satisfying and acceptable; for others it leads to real trouble in the form of jealousy, distrust, guilt, and shame.

Some people are now saying that partnerships—married or unmarried—should not be exclusive. They believe that while a primary relationship is maintained with one person, the freedom for both partners to love and share sex with others should always be present. Reasons given for seeing outside sexual contacts as desirable include the need for sexual variety, the belief that one other person cannot satisfy all of the sexual needs of some individuals, and special situations such as the married partners being apart for extended periods of time. These more open sexual relationships may be possible for some people, but most cannot handle the hurt and jealousy well. One difficulty experienced by many is that working at love and successful sex with more than one person at a time takes more energy, and this makes it hard to balance things out without someone getting hurt.

Again, however, it is important to emphasize that each couple will have to resolve for themselves the issue of whether or not to be sexually exclusive for each other. There is no general statement that can be made here about the "best" or "healthiest" way to be. Two partners who care about one another will approach such questions with honesty and try to work them out in such a way that fits best with the feelings, values, and needs of both. Neither partner should feel persuaded into a pattern of relationships which is uncomfortable or hurtful for anyone involved.

### Some Experimental Partnerships

In recent years, several books and magazine articles have dealt with the new types of marriages and other partnerships that a few couples are attempting. For the most part, it is too soon to evaluate how successful these experimental partnerships tend to be. While most experts seem to feel that there can be the dangers of very negative consequences, some are indicating that a few couples can probably handle such relationships quite well. We'll take a very brief look at these experiments.

*Open marriage* is the name given to marriages in which the husband and wife allow one another to have outside friendships, quite independently of each other. These friendships may or may not include sexual contact. In those cases where the partners routinely have sexual relationships with others, it is sometimes called a *comarriage.* The two partners live quite separate lives, although they return to the primary relationship and share living quarters whenever they wish. *Swinging* or *mate-swapping* refers to married couples who occasionally seek out sexual contact with other partners. In some areas, there are clubs which bring couples together who are interested in "swapping." Other times, swapping happens between couples who are friends and gradually become involved sexually. As we explored in the preceding section of this chapter, such behavior can lead to serious problems for a marriage, and the decisions must be approached with honesty, caring, and extreme caution. Some husbands and wives seek extramarital sex as an escape from unhappiness or dissatisfaction with their marriages. In these cases, outside activity may well further weaken the partnership and lead to a break-up of the marriage.

A few professionals have recommended the establishment of *trial marriage.* In such an arrangement, a couple interested in marriage would agree, with legal bonds, to be married for a short length of time, such as two years. Then, if the trial marriage is successful and both partners still wish to continue in it, they would enter into a more permanent marriage. If not, the relationship is dissolved with no further legal obligations. Part of the agreement would be not to have any children during the trial marriage, by using effective birth control methods.

### Marriage Contracts

Another innovative approach to marriage has been the writing of a formal *marriage contract*. Some couples have worked out in detail what the duties, rights, and responsibilities of each partner should be, and have written up a formal contract. These couples feel that there is less chance for misunderstandings and problems later if such things are decided upon ahead of time. There is still some question as to how binding such documents can actually be on the marriage partners, but some lawyers are encouraging couples to go ahead with the writing of a contract if they wish.

### The Future of Marriage

Most experts agree that marriage—in some form or another—will be around for a long time. Statistics show that most divorced people remarry, and that more people are getting married than ever before.

Some observers of social patterns believe that marriage partnerships will gradually become less exclusive, and that we shall see an increase in open marriages, comarriages, trial marriages, and mate-swapping. Others feel that there will be a shift toward people having more than one marriage during a lifetime, or that such a series of committed relationships will become the pattern, without formal, legalized marriage. There are still others who believe that we may have a shift back toward exclusive closed marriages which last for a lifetime. Only time will reveal which predictions are correct.

Regardless of whether or not it is written down as a formal legal document, every decision to enter a committed relationship represents a contract. It is a contract between two human beings who are committing themselves to deeper levels of sharing. Each partner promises to participate in the positive and negative aspects of that commitment. Before taking the step toward marriage, it is important for both individuals to consider fully what that commitment means to their lives and exactly what kinds of promises they are ready to make to each other. Many couples could benefit from premarital counseling, so that they may talk through these important issues with a trusted counselor. Another issue to be considered is parenthood, discussed in the next chapter.

**Partnerships and Your Life**

1. Think about the following questions and decide where you stand right now in your life. During the next few years, some of your values may change, but try to focus in on what you believe at present.

   a. Do you expect to marry some day? Why or why not?
   b. Of the married couples you know, which have the relationship(s) that seem most appealing to you? Think about those couples: What are the characteristics of each individual which seem to make the marriages "work"?
   c. How important do you think sex should be in a marriage?

2. *Marriage Contract*

   a. On the next page are portions of a few articles from an actual marriage contract which one couple in Seattle, Washington, developed before they married. See what you think of it:

---

MARRIAGE CONTRACT[1]
OF
HARRIETT M. CODY AND HARVEY J. SADIS

*Article I. Names.* Harriett and Harvey affirm their individuality and equality in this relationship. . . . Therefore they agree to retain and use the given family names of each party. The Parties will employ the titles of address, Ms. Cody and Mr. Sadis.

*Article II. Relationships with Others.* The Parties agree to allow each other as much time with other friends individually as they spend with each other. The Parties freely acknowledge their insecurities about sexual relationships beyond the partnership. Therefore, they agree to maintain sexual fidelity to each other.

---

[1]Copyright *Ms. Magazine,* 1975. Reprinted with permission.

*Article IV.  Children.*  The Parties agree that any children will
be the result of choice, not chance, and therefore the decision to have children will be mutual and deliberate. Further,
the Parties agree that the responsibility for birth control will
be shared.

*Article V.  Careers.*  Harriett and Harvey value the importance
and integrity of their respective careers. . . . Commitment to
their careers will sometimes place stress on the relationship.
Yet, insofar as their careers contribute to individual self-ful-
fillment, the careers strengthen the partnership.

*Article VI.  Care and Use of Living Space.*  The Parties agree
to share equally in the performance of all household tasks,
taking into consideration individual schedules and preferences. Periodic allocation of household tasks will be made,
in which the time involved in the performance of each
party's tasks is equal. . . . Each party shall have an individual area within the home in an equal amount, insofar as
space is available.

---

b.  Now, here is a list of some of the things Harriett and
Harvey wanted for their marriage. Check whether or
not each item would be important for you:

| I would want this | I would *not* want this | Undecided | |
|---|---|---|---|
| ___ | ___ | ___ | The wife keeps her own last name, instead of taking the husband's last name. |
| ___ | ___ | ___ | The freedom for *both* partners to spend as much time with their own friends as they do with each other. |
| ___ | ___ | ___ | Sexual fidelity (having sexual relations only with each other). |
| ___ | ___ | ___ | Deciding when to have children will be a mutual responsibility of both partners. |
| ___ | ___ | ___ | Both partners may pursue their own careers outside the home if they wish. |

Both partners share equally in all household tasks.

If space is available, both partners will have their own separate areas to use as they wish.

3.  What kind of partner do you want?

a.  Consider the following list of personal qualities and characteristics. Pick out the 10 which seem most important to you in a partner:

Good-looking face
Attractive body
Good cook
Intelligent
Good education
Gentle and kind
Has plenty of money
Honest and sincere
Unemotional and controlled
Places few demands on you
Likes travel and excitement
Good house-keeper
Independent spirit
Quiet and a little shy
Enjoys parties and entertaining
Has same interests as you

Likes children
Has a good job
Good sex partner
Dependent on you
Gets along well with others
Less intelligent than you
Wants a nice home
Will allow you sexual freedom
Aggressive go-getter
Wants to communicate
Shows emotions
Has different interests from you
Does not want children
Wants a simple life
Other. _____
_____

b.  Now, think about the 10 qualities you have chosen. Assign them each a number from 1 to 10, 1 being the most important to you, and 10 being the least important to you.

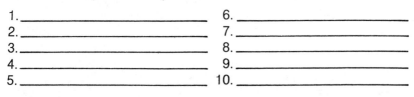

1._____     6. _____
2._____     7. _____
3._____     8. _____
4._____     9. _____
5._____    10. _____

**For Further Reading**

Calderone, Mary S. and Editors of Bride's Magazine. *Questions and Answers About Love and Sex*. New York: Avon Books, 1979.

Leslie, Gerald R. and Leslie, Elizabeth M. *Marriage in a Changing World*. New York: John Wiley and Sons, 1977.

Libby, Roger W. and Whitehurst, Robert N. *Marriage and Alternatives: Exploring Intimate Relationships*. Glenview, IL: Scott, Foresman, 1977.

Nass, Gilbert D.; Libby, Roger W.; and Fisher, Mary Pat. *Sexual Choices*. Florence, KY: Wadsworth Publishing, 1984.

Richards, Arlene and Willis, Ilene. *How to Get it Together When Your Parents are Coming Apart*. New York: Bantam Books, 1977.

Rosenberg, Ellen. *Growing Up Feeling Good*. New York: Beaufort Books, 1983.

# 10    A Parent: To Be or Not To Be

This chapter is about having children and being a parent, and not having children. Having a baby is indeed a miraculous process, although there is no special trick to it. Most men and women have the capability of creating a new human being. With the effective methods of birth control now available, all men and women also have the capability of preventing the development of a child. Parenthood is a more complicated issue. Being a good parent doesn't just happen; it requires certain qualities and it means working on the development of certain attitudes.

The decision to have a child must be approached with caution and careful thought. Child-raising requires much attention, time, and money. Children need parents who can provide love, security, and good models for reaching responsible adulthood. Parents are the ones who give personalities and values to the next generation, and that is a big responsibility not only to the children, but to society.

The majority of children are raised within a marriage, although more all the time are growing up in families where their natural parents do not live together. It is still accepted that marriage is a good relationship for raising children, because many people believe it provides increased security and stability. When the marriage is based on love, children can be exposed to the warmth and caring so necessary for their well-being. Of course, a poor marriage—where love, security, and warmth are not available—may be harmful to children. Undoubtedly some children are better off after a divorce than before. It is also recognized today that many unmarried couples and single people can be good, nurturing parents and provide good homes for children. There is bound to be more work for a single parent than for a parent who can share the job of parenting.

### What Makes a "Good Parent"?

There is a great deal of disagreement on the "best" ways to raise children. Like everything else, the qualities each individual parent displays depend on all of the other aspects of his or her personality. Yet, there seem to be some fundamental characteristics essential to effective parenthood:

1. *A desire to have children.* It helps to want children and to like them. When children are unexpected, unwanted, or considered a nuisance, they are bound to create tension.

2. *Security and stability.* Children tend to grow up healthy and happy when they are given a basic security and stability. This doesn't mean plenty of money, but instead it means a feeling of strength and consistency from their parents. This not only helps them trust the world around them, but helps them to trust themselves.

3. *Warmth, trust, and respect.* Children depend on their parents for many things, including food and shelter. Most psychologists agree that they also depend on their parents—during their early years—for human warmth and caring. Children need to feel loved and worth loving. Parents also must try to trust their children and respect them as individuals.

4. *Sharing and communicating.* Parents are people, too, and children need to share in their feelings, ideas, and values. Likewise, children need to be able to let parents know what is going on inside. It's up to parents to set the climate where two-way communication can happen. Good listening on the part of the parent is an important part of that climate.

5. *Setting Rules.* Younger children need to know the limits that they have. Parents have the difficult responsibility of establishing fair rules, setting good examples for their children, and being fair about enforcing the rules.

There are plenty of other qualities which could be mentioned. One thing is certain: being a good parent is one of the most difficult, time-consuming jobs that human beings ever have. In today's society, it also takes a great deal of money. Experts tell us that the annual cost of raising one child is between ten and twenty percent of the family's income. So, it all adds up to the fact that parenthood should be a decision reached with great care. In the next section, we'll take a look at how a new human being is created.

### Conception—The Beginning

Several times in earlier chapters, we have talked about our sexual feelings and their importance to our lives. One of the important functions of our sex organs is *reproduction*—producing more of our species. Be sure you understand the anatomy of the reproductive systems described in Chapter Two before you try to understand how reproduction occurs.

Remember that the male's testes produce millions of microscopic, swimming *sperm*. The sperm are suspended in the *semen,* which the male ejaculates when he experiences orgasm or sexual climax. The female's ovaries produce *eggs* or *ova,* usually one about every month. After the egg or *ovum* has broken through the wall of the ovary at ovulation, it moves along through the fallopian tube for two or three days.

During sexual intercourse, the semen may be ejaculated from the erect penis of the male into the vagina of the female. Gradually, the semen seeps through the opening of the cervix and into the uterus. The millions of sperm in the semen move their tails and swim further into the female reproductive organs. Sperm can probably live from three to five days within the female reproductive system. Eventually, they reach the fallopian tubes. If an ovum is present in one of the tubes, one of the sperm may penetrate the outer wall of the ovum and enter it. This is called *fertilization* or *conception,* and a pregnancy has begun. As soon as the sperm has fertilized the ovum, a change occurs in the ovum's outer layers so that no more sperm may enter.

It is sometimes possible for pregnancy to occur even if actual sexual intercourse has not occurred. If, during petting or sex play, the male ejaculates semen near the opening of the vagina, it is possible for some of the semen to get into the vagina. The sperm in the semen may fertilize the ovum. Remember—although the more sperm present, the more likelihood of fertilization, it only takes *one* sperm to fertilize an ovum. Some couples make the mistake of thinking that if the male withdraws his penis before ejaculating, pregnancy cannot result. Actually, the clear fluid from Cowper's glands, which comes out of the penis during sexual arousal, may carry some sperm and therefore have the possibility of pregnancy.

### Implantation in the Uterus

Soon after the ovum has been fertilized, it begins the process of cell division. It divides first to form two cells; then both of these divide, forming four cells. The cells continue to divide until a spherical mass of cells has formed. The entire mass of cells is no bigger than the tiny ovum was before fertilization.

All of this cell division takes place as the fertilized ovum continues to move down the fallopian tubes and into the uterus. After seven or eight days, the mass of cells becomes attached to the inner wall of the uterus and produces special enzymes that help it to dissolve some of the uterine lining. Gradually, it buries itself within the lining. This is called *implantation.* (see figure 10.1)

The cells of the developing *embryo* absorb food from the surrounding tissues of the uterus and begin to grow. Cell division continues until three layers gradually form the developing baby's organs. One layer becomes the nervous system, skin, sense organs, and mouth. Another layer becomes the respiratory and digestive systems. The third layer develops into muscles, bones, blood vessels, and sex organs.

While the embryo is growing and developing, special membranes form around it. One is a tough sac around the embryo, filled with fluid. This is the *amnion* or "bag of waters." The amnion provides a moist cushion that protects the embryo suspended in it.

Another structure that forms along the uterine lining as the embryo grows is the *placenta.* The embryo eventually is connected to the placenta by its *umbilical cord.* These are important structures for bringing nourishment to the developing embryo.

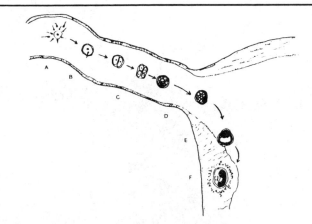

**Figure 10.1** Fertilization and implantation. The ovum is surrounded by sperm (A) and is eventually fertilized by one sperm (B). It then begins to divide (C). For several days, cell division continues (D) as the developing embryo moves into the uterus. Within 7 or 8 days, the mass of cells has made contact with the uterine wall (E), and gradually becomes implanted there (F).

Blood vessels from the embryo connect to special vessels leading through the umbilical cord into the placenta and back again. They come very close to blood vessels from the mother's body which extend into the placenta. The blood of the embryo and its mother come very close together, but they do not mix (Figure 10.2). However, they are close enough so that oxygen and nutrients enter the embryo's bloodstream. Also, waste products from the embryo leave its blood and pass into the mother's body. Her kidneys and lungs then get rid of the waste products. The lungs, digestive system, and kidneys of the embryo do not need to function fully until after birth. The placenta gets larger as the developing baby grows until at the time of birth, the placenta is a large roundish mass of tissue, several inches in diameter and more than an inch thick. The umbilical cord grows to a length of about twenty inches.

### Boy or Girl and How Many?

It is the *chromosomes*, present in the cells of the embryo, that determine almost all of the physical characteristics of the

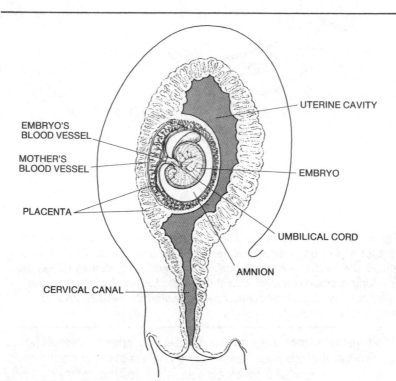

**Figure 10.2** Blood vessels from the embryo travel through the umbilical cord into the placenta, where they come very near the blood vessels of the mother. Although the 2 blood systems do not mix, they are close enough so that materials may be exchanged between them.

new human being: its eventual size and bone structure; the color of its skin, eyes, and hair; its sex; and everything else. Both the sperm and ovum contain 23 chromosomes each. When fertilization occurs, these sets of chromosomes combine to form 46. As cell division proceeds and the embryo grows, each new cell gets a full set of 46 chromosomes.

Since the embryo gets half of its chromosomes from the mother and half from the father, its characteristics will be a blend of the traits carried by those chromosomes. Which traits show themselves and which do not are explained by the science of *genetics,* not covered in this book.

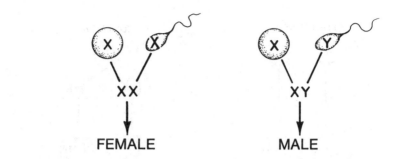

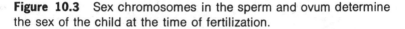

**Figure 10.3** Sex chromosomes in the sperm and ovum determine the sex of the child at the time of fertilization.

The sex of a child—whether it will be a boy or girl—is determined at the moment of fertilization. The ovum carries one chromosome that helps determine the sex of the embryo; it is called the *X chromosome.* Sperm also carry one sex-determining chromosome, but they may carry either an *X chromosome* or a *Y chromosome.* If a sperm which fertilizes the ovum carries an X chromosome, it combines with the ovum's X,. and forms a female (XX). If the sperm carries a Y chromosome, the XY combination forms a male (see figure 10.3). Although the infant's sex is determined at fertilization, the actual sex organs do not become visible until late in the third month of development.

Multiple births—twins, triplets, and so on—also are formed very early in development. *Fraternal twins* are the result of the ovaries producing two separate eggs or ova, both of which are fertilized by separate sperm. These twins may be the same or opposite sex and look no more alike than any other children in the family might be expected to look. *Identical twins,* however, result from a single ovum being fertilized by a single sperm. When the fertilized ovum divides for the first time, the two new cells separate completely, each developing into an embryo. Since their cells carry identical chromosomes, their physical traits are also identical (Figure 10.4). Triplets may be formed by fertilization of 3 separate ova, or two ova, one splitting at the first cell division. Other multiple births involve similar combinations.

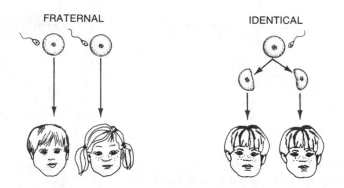

**Figure 10.4** Twins are either fraternal, formed from two separate ova fertilized by two separate sperm; or identical, formed from one ovum fertilized by one sperm, then dividing.

### Fetal Development

From fertilization to birth, nine months are required for development of the fetus to the extent that it can survive outside of the uterus. A baby which is born before the full nine months are completed is said to be *premature*. The earlier it is born, the less chance of survival. Babies born during the seventh month have a better than 50% chance of living. Most babies born during the eighth or ninth month survive. Fewer babies born before the seventh month live, although larger medical centers have neonatal intensive care units that are now greatly increasing their chances of survival.

After the embryo has been growing and developing for two months, it is usually called a *fetus*. Tremendous changes occur in the fetus as it begins to take on the characteristics of a human being. By the time it is born, the fetus weighs *6 billion times* more than when it was a fertilized ovum. There are few identifiable human characteristics until the third month of pregnancy. By then, the fetus is two to three inches in length, and fingers, toes, and facial features are visible. As Figure 10.5 shows, the fetus gradually looks more and more like a human being as growth and development continue.

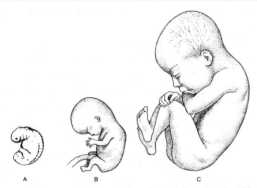

**Figure 10.5**  Many changes occur as the fetus develops. (A) Embryo at 4 weeks, about 1/12 inch in length; (B) Fetus at 8½ weeks, 1 inch long, weighing 1/15 ounce; (C) The fetus at 16 weeks, about 8 inches long and weighing about 6 ounces. By this time, the movements of the fetus may be felt and its heartbeat detected with a stethoscope.

### Signs and Limitations of Pregnancy

When a woman is pregnant, the first possible indications include not experiencing menstruation, nausea and vomiting in the morning, fatigue, changes in the size and fullness of the breasts, and more frequent urination. Of course, these symptoms may have other causes too, or may not appear during pregnancy.

There are several tests that physicians can administer to determine whether or not a woman is pregnant. Home pregnancy test kits are also widely available in drug stores, without prescription. The most accurate of these do-it-yourself tests are the "monoclonal" tests, that look for a specific hormone. If the test is positive, indicating pregnancy, a physician or family planning clinic should be consulted. Often, the test will be repeated there to confirm the pregnancy.

The clinician will also do an internal examination, looking for changes in the cervix and size of the uterus. A mucus plug appears in the opening of the cervix that apparently prevents germs and other material from entering the uterus and endangering the embryo. Signs that are detected later in pregnancy are the movements of the fetus and hearing the fetal heartbeat with a stethoscope. The fetal skeleton may also be seen in an Xray or its outline shown in a special sound wave picture called a sonagram.

A healthy pregnant woman is encouraged to pursue her normal activities. Unless the physician recommends it; there is no reason to limit travel, exercise, or sexual activity during pregnancy. In the last four to six weeks before birth, sexual intercourse may become difficult because of the woman's large abdomen, but different positions for intercourse sometimes are successful. Some couples use other forms of sexual gratification—such as mutual masturbation—during the final weeks of pregnancy.

### The Birth Process
After the nine months of development, the baby is born. Childbirth is a process about which there is a great deal of misunderstanding and unnecessary fear. For pregnant women who are helped to understand what will happen when their child is born, the birth process can become a cooperative effort among herself, trained medical professionals, and her partner. It need not be a frightening and painful mystery.

There are three signs that can indicate that the birth process is starting. The most common signal is the beginning of powerful muscle contractions called *labor* in the uterus. At first, the contractions occur every 15 to 20 minutes, and last about 30 seconds each. Gradually, the labor contractions become stronger and occur more frequently, until they are coming every 3 to 4 minutes. Labor usually lasts between 8 and 20 hours. Each uterine contraction moves the fetus farther down toward the vagina. The opening in the cervix gradually widens to a diameter of about 4 inches.

The second sign that may appear early in the birth process is the expelling of the mucus plug from the opening to the uterus. Another sign may be the breaking of the amnion, or bag of waters, so that the fluid which protects the baby flows out of the vagina. Sometimes, the amnion does not break until much later in labor.

When the opening of the cervix is completely open, the fetus slowly moves into the vagina, now called the *birth canal*. The vagina is capable of stretching a great deal to accommodate the

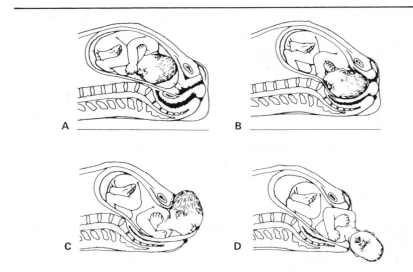

**Figure 10.6** The Birth Process. (A) The fetus inside the uterus as the birth process begins. (B) The cervix has widened and the baby moves through the birth canal. (C) The baby's head becomes visible in the vaginal opening. (D) The baby's body turns and one shoulder emerges. (From *Human Sexuality* by James Leslie McCary, copyright 1978 by Litton Educational Publishing, Inc. Reprinted by permission of D. Van Nostrand Company)

emerging baby. The fetus is usually in a head-first position (see Figure 10.6). Occasionally a fetus is in a backward or sideways position and may require special attention from the physician delivering it, usually an *obstetrician*. An hour or two is normally required for the fetus to move through the birth canal.

If delivery of the baby occurs in the hospital, the mother is usually placed on the delivery table, with her knees bent and thighs wide apart. As the baby's head emerges through the opening to the vagina, the mother's tissues must stretch a great deal. Sometimes, the obstetrician will make a small cut to widen the opening, so that tearing will not occur. During the latter stages of birth, it is important for the mother to help push the baby out by contracting her abdominal muscles. Once the infant's head has fully emerged, its body turns to the right or left.

The physician then helps guide the shoulders out. The remainder of the baby's body emerges easily and rapidly (see Figure 10.6).

The umbilical cord is still attached to the baby after birth. The obstetrician ties the cord in two places and cuts it close to the infant's body. Whatever is left will eventually fall off, leaving the navel or "belly button." About 15 minutes following the baby's birth, the placenta—left inside the uterus—along with the remaining portion of umbilical cord, are also expelled from the uterus through the vagina. This process is sometimes called the *afterbirth*.

Giving birth to a baby is hard work and involves some pain at various stages of labor and delivery. Many women now participate in classes to prepare for childbirth. The father of the baby, or someone else close to the mother, takes the same classes to learn how to be a "coach" during labor and delivery. They learn relaxation and breathing techniques to relieve some discomfort of labor contractions, and also practice the pushing movements necessary to delivery of the baby. Most hospitals now allow the father, or other coach, to be present for the entire birth process.

If there is some problem with the normal birth process described above, the obstetrician or surgeon may have to perform a special operation called a *caesarean section*. In this procedure, a cut is made in the abdomen and through the uterus, and the baby is removed from the uterus through the cut. The term caesarean section originated from the legend that Julius Caesar was brought into the world in this manner.

Once the child has been born, the difficult process of parenting must begin. In fact, there is increasing research evidence to indicate that loving contact between the parents and the newborn baby is extremely important even in the first hour or two after it is born. There may be a process of *bonding* that occurs between parents and their children during that period. The cycle of human life continues, with the process of reproduction as its principal source of inertia.

### Not Having Children
It is apparent that many couples have children for the wrong reasons. Every couple must think carefully about their reasons

for having children, and be cautious that they have not been trapped into some of these wrong reasons:

1. *Because young couples are "supposed" to have children.* Many married couples get pressure from their parents and others to hurry up and have children, even before they have had sufficient time to adjust to one another. Studies show that it is often wise to wait until later in the marriage before the extra pressures and problems of children are created. In fact, there are some couples who never want to have children, and they are able to lead happy, fulfilled lives together.

2. *To "strengthen" the marriage.* Some couples who are having trouble with their marriages decide that having a child may patch things up. Actually, pregnancy and giving birth may bring the couples closer together temporarily, but if their deeper problems are not worked out, they are bound to re-appear later on. Then, the child may only add to the difficulties and be affected by them. Remember—babies aren't marriage counselors.

3. *Because babies and children are so cute and fun to have around.* They may be just that much of the time, but they also take a lot of work, energy, and money. And as they get older, they often are rebellious and uncooperative. They sometimes get sick. Anyone who looks only at the positive aspects of kids is probably being unrealistic.

So, there may be plenty of good reasons for a couple to delay having children until *they* are ready, or not to have children at all. Some couples decide to adopt children rather than have their own, since there are so many youngsters who need good homes.

### Family Planning

Most professionals agree that successful marriage and successful parenthood are helped along by careful planning of the family. That means deciding when to start having children, how many to have, and how often to have them, in light of the family's financial situation and the readiness of the parents.

Several research studies indicate that children and their parents tend to be happier and better adjusted when there are fewer, well-spaced children. The myths about the spoiled only child are not supported by facts either. Studies show that only children often are physically and mentally healthier, and achieve greater success in later life than children who have brothers and sisters.

Successful family planning will depend on the use of methods of *birth control,* or *contraception.* Responsible sex between a woman and a man must include the use of birth control methods whenever there is the risk of an unwanted pregnancy. It should also be noted that pregnancy *can* occur whenever sexual intercourse occurs, even with contraceptive protection. Contraception greatly reduces the chances of pregnancy, but cannot eliminate them. Some methods of contraception are more effective and reliable than others. Any partners who are really ready to share sexual intercourse should be ready to discuss birth control and to decide together which method(s) they wish to use. The following sections of this chapter provide more information on the various methods.

### Types of Birth Control

One method of birth control is *abstinence*—not participating in sexual intercourse. Some couples make this choice, especially unmarried couples. They may substitute other forms of sexual activity for intercourse.

For couples who choose to have sexual intercourse, yet wish to delay children until later in their lives, there are several ways of preventing fertilization. One of the most widely used methods, though not particularly reliable, is *withdrawal of the penis* from the vagina before ejaculation. Through the years, several methods have been developed to *prevent the sperm from reaching the ovum.* These include use of the *condom,* the *diaphragm,* and *chemicals that kill sperm* (spermicides).

Through changing hormone levels in the female's body, the *ovum may be prevented from leaving the ovary.* The *birth control pill,* and several other hormonal methods, work this way. Another device is the *intrauterine device (IUD),* although the manner in which it prevents pregnancy is poorly understood. Some couples attempt to have sexual intercourse during times in the woman's menstrual cycle when the ovum is not likely to be in the fallopian tubes. This is called *natural family planning/fertility awareness.* Each of these methods will be discussed in more detail:

*Withdrawal of the Penis* from the vagina before ejaculation is obviously a very unreliable method of birth control, although some couples manage to use it successfully. One danger is that sperm may be present in the Cowper's gland fluid which comes out of the penis *before* ejaculation. A further disadvantage is that it requires careful control and attention by the male partner. He must "stay tuned in" to himself so that he knows when ejaculation is about to occur, and then pull out in time. Some men find this difficult or impossible, regardless of their good intentions. Many couples feel that the need for such control does not permit relaxed, enjoyable sex. Statistics show a high failure rate for this method, so it is one of the more unreliable methods for preventing pregnancy. It is however, better than using no method of birth control at all.

*The Condom* ("rubber," "safe," "prophylactic") is placed on the penis before intercourse begins and worn during intercourse. Its function is to collect the semen when ejaculation occurs, so that it does not enter the vagina. Most condoms are made of very thin rubber which does not interfere with the sensations of sex, although more expensive condoms made of animal membranes are also available (sometimes called "skins").

Condoms are available in most drug stores, and no doctor's prescription is needed. The most reliable condoms are individually wrapped. They are rolled into a ring which is then unrolled out onto the erect penis. Some condoms have a small space

**Figure 10.7**  The condom: rolled; unrolled; unrolled on the erect penis, with space at the tip to collect semen.

built-in at the end for collection of the semen. If such a space is not built-in, a small amount of space should be left at the tip of the condom for the semen. While the condom is being unrolled onto the penis, the space at its end should be pinched so that it will not even contain air (see Figure 10.7).

The two main dangers when using the condom are breakage and slippage. It is possible for a condom to break during intercourse or to slip off the penis, especially after ejaculation when the penis begins to lose its erection. Occasional checking of the condom during intercourse is wise, and when the penis is withdrawn, the *condom should be held on* with the fingers so that it does not slip off in the vagina. Rubber condoms become weakened easily, and should *not* be stored in a warm place such as a wallet or glove compartment in a car. Some condoms are lubricated to make entry into the vagina easier. Petroleum jellies, such as Vaseline, will dissolve the rubber, causing breakage of a condom.

The effectiveness of condoms is improved when used with a sperm-killing chemical. A further advantage of the condom is that it offers good protection against the spread of sexually transmitted diseases.

*Chemicals which Kill Sperm* or *Spermicides* come in the form of creams, jellies, foams, or suppositories. They should be inserted into the vagina, as directed on the package, *immediately before each intercourse.* Their failure rate when used alone is high so they are *better used along with the condom or diaphragm.* They prevent fertilization by helping to block the entrance to the uterus so that semen does not enter it and by killing the sperm. These chemicals are also available without prescription in drug stores. A relatively new method of contraception is the *birth control sponge*, available without prescription. They are placed over the cervix at the back of the vagina, and contain a spermicidal chemical.

*The Diaphragm* is a cup of thin rubber, stretched over a ring, which is inserted with the fingers into the vagina and placed over the cervix of the uterus (see Figure 10.8). A sperm-killing cream or jelly is placed on the diaphragm to make it more effective. A diaphragm must be fitted for a woman by a trained medical person. It is inserted into the vagina within 6 hours before inter-

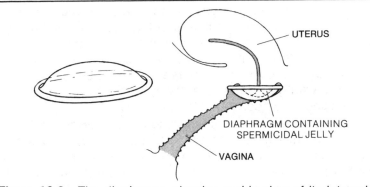

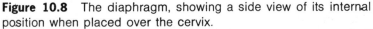

**Figure 10.8** The diaphragm, showing a side view of its internal position when placed over the cervix.

course, and then should not be removed until at least 6 hours after intercourse, although it may be left in for up to 24 hours. Used with spermicidal jelly, the diaphragm is very effective.

The Pill is a form of oral contraception, since the pills are taken by mouth. Birth control pills contain hormones that prevent ovulation, the releasing of an ovum by the ovaries. If the ovum is not present in the female's fallopian tubes, fertilization cannot occur.

There are several different types of birth control pills, and a physician must weigh factors of age and health in deciding whether it is a suitable method of birth control and which type should be prescribed. Then, the pills must be taken faithfully as directed. In one method they are begun on the fifth day of the menstrual cycle, counting from the first day of menstruation. Then, a pill is taken each day for another 20 days, and for the following 5 or 6 days no pills are taken. In another method, a pill is taken every day. If pills are skipped, the risk of pregnancy increases.

There is a great deal of controversy over the use of The Pill, since there is a possibility of some unpleasant side effects. Recent research has shown that women over 35 and those who smoke should not use the pill because of the increased risk of side effects. However, the consensus seems to be that when prescribed and used under the careful supervision of a physician, the risks of birth control pills are lower than the risks accompanying pregnancy. Myths about the pill's dangers have developed over the years, but research tends to show that it is a relatively safe form of contraception. It even has been shown to help prevent certain types of ovarian and uterine cancer. The more carelessly it is used, of course, the more chance of pregnancy or unwanted side effects. If any side effects appear, the physician should be consulted immediately.

Some girls have made the mistake of "borrowing" birth control pills from their mother or a friend. This is a dangerous practice since the pills have not been properly prescribed for them. Some have mistakenly believed that *one pill* will do the job, often with the result of pregnancy.

*The Intrauterine Device* (IUD) became available around 1960. IUDs have been made in a variety of shapes, usually out of flexible plastic or metal (see Figure 10.9). The IUD is inserted by a family planning clinician directly into the uterus. A fine thread extends out into the vagina so that the woman or her partner can check occasionally to make sure the IUD is still in place.

There is disagreement as to how the IUD actually works. The most widely accepted idea is that the device somehow interferes with the implantation of an embryo in the wall of the uterus.

Some women experience some discomfort after an IUD has been inserted, and there is a chance of the uterus expelling the device. When pregnancy is desired, the IUD must be removed

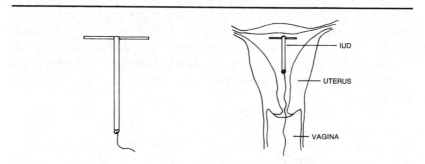

**Figure 10.9**  An IUD, shown in place inside the uterus. An IUD must be inserted by a clinician.

by a qualified professional. Because there is an increased risk of infection with IUDs, most types have been withdrawn from the market. This method is, for the most part, unavailable to younger women.

*Natural Family Planning/Fertility Awareness* involves careful attention to the woman's menstrual cycle so that sexual intercourse does not take place where the ovum is present and may be fertilized. It is a "natural" method of birth control considered acceptable to the Roman Catholic Church. Typically, women experience ovulation 14 to 16 days before their next menstrual period is to begin. At that time, the ovum is present in the fallopian tubes for about 3 days and could be fertilized. So for a few days before, during, and after that time, sexual intercourse could lead to pregnancy and is avoided, or other forms of birth control are used. The difficult part of this method is determining when ovulation takes place. Again, this is best figured out with the aid of a family planning specialist, who will help the woman keep careful records of her menstrual cycle over a period of several months. This part of the method has been called the *rhythm method,* and is not considered very reliable when used alone. However, natural family planning uses two additional methods of determining when ovulation occurs. The *basal temperature method,* for example, uses measures of body temperature to help pinpoint when ovulation takes place. The *cervical mucus method* requires regular checking of the consistency of mucus around the cervix, at the back of the vagina. This consistency changes around the time of ovulation.

There are a number of potential problems with this method. For those girls and women whose menstrual cycles are irregular and vary in length from month to month, predicting ovulation may be difficult. Natural family planning/fertility awareness is most likely to be successful when used by couples living together in a stable relationship where their life cycles are reasonably predictable and the commitment to cooperating together on the method is strong. Since it is a complicated method, it is best taught by a qualified professional.

*Sterilization* is a procedure by which a man or woman is made incapable of reproducing. More and more people—especially after having a certain number of children—are choosing to be sterilized. Women are usually sterilized by a cutting and/or tying of the fallopian tubes. Physicians are also experimenting with plugs that can be inserted in the fallopian tubes, and then removed when pregnancy is desired. Other more complicated surgery that involves removal of the ovaries or uterus also leads to sterilization, though it would not be done solely for that purpose. The most common method for male sterilization is a simple procedure called a *vasectomy,* in which the vas deferens—the tube which leads sperm upward from the testes—is cut and tied. Although these sterilization procedures are sometimes reversible, they should be considered relatively permanent. Therefore, if there is any possibility of an individual desiring children at a later time, they should not be employed.

New forms of birth control are being developed through research, and more reliable, convenient techniques may soon be available. Women can be given *injections* of a hormone that will prevent ovulation for three months. There is also a hormone-releasing *implant* that is placed under the skin of the forearm. It then slowly releases a hormone for up to five years. The Federal Food and Drug Administration has recently approved a *vaginal contraceptive film,* a papery substance with a spermicidal chemical, placed at the back of the vagina prior to intercourse.

There has been a good deal of discussion about birth control pills for men that would cause temporary sterility. Such a pill would either prevent production of sperm in the testes or inactivate the sperm in some way. Researchers report that the pill for males is still a fair distance away, and marketing studies indicate that men will be reluctant to take it.

### Birth Control that Doesn't Work

In the past, many myths have developed about methods of birth control. Except for the techniques described earlier, these methods can be expected to have little, if any, effectiveness. One old and ineffective method is *douching,* washing out the vagina after intercourse. A variety of douches have been suggested, including various kinds of soft drinks such as Coca-Cola. These do not wash the sperm out and prevent pregnancy. Most physicians agree that douching usually serves no useful function unless prescribed for a vaginal infection, and may actually harm the linings of the vagina. The vaginal sprays sold in stores are for perfuming purposes only and *not* for birth control.

Another myth holds that if the woman does not reach orgasm, she cannot become pregnant. Ovulation has nothing to do with orgasm, so there is just as much chance for pregnancy with or without orgasm. Having intercourse during the woman's menstrual period, when the menstrual flow is present, also offers no guarantee that pregnancy will not occur.

It is also not true that pregnancy cannot occur the first time a girl experiences intercourse. Pregnancy can indeed result from the first intercourse.

### Unwanted Pregnancy

Some young people make the mistake of thinking "it couldn't happen to me." They fool themselves into thinking that "just once won't matter," or believe the silly myths about pregnancy. The fact remains that *any time sexual intercourse takes place, there is some risk of pregnancy.* Even the most reliable methods of birth control can fail, resulting in an unwanted pregnancy. So, any couple choosing to share sex should think and talk about what they might do should an unwanted pregnancy occur.

This can be a very difficult problem, with many feelings and decisions to be faced. Talking things over with a good counselor may be important. Briefly, there are three main options available. One is to keep the baby. This choice necessitates decisions about whether or not the couple will marry, who will actually raise the child, whether or not the parents' education can continue, and so on. A second option is to have the baby and offer it for adoption. Most adoption agencies have long lists of couples hoping to be able to adopt babies. The third option is to end the pregnancy through induced abortion, explained in the next section.

### Abortion

*Abortion* refers to the expulsion of a growing embryo or fetus from the uterus, thus ending the pregnancy before the baby is born. This sometimes occurs as the result of natural causes, and is then called a *spontaneous abortion* or *miscarriage.*

There are also methods by which a physician can induce abortion. In years past, when induced abortion was illegal except for very special cases, many pregnant girls and women sought illegal abortions from untrained persons. These dangerous procedures often led to injury, disease, or even death. As the result of new state laws and a 1973 Supreme Court decision, safe and legal abortions by qualified physicians may be obtained in many areas. There are many individuals and some religious and political groups who object to abortion on moral grounds, insisting that it is tantamount to killing another human being. An opposite point of view is that a fetus is part of a woman's body and that the woman should have the right to decide whether or not she wishes to give birth to the child. Most professionals agree that effective contraception is certainly better than having to resort to an abortion, but abortion is an option that many pregnant women still wish to choose.

Abortions may be induced several ways by a physician, although this is best done during the first trimester, or first three months of pregnancy. Most methods involve the insertion of some instrument into the uterus which evacuates the uterine contents. In later weeks of pregnancy, it may be necessary to inject a saline solution into the uterus causing eventual expulsion of the fetus from the uterus. When done by a properly trained physician, an abortion—especially during the early weeks—can be done safely, quickly, without much discomfort, and at a cost of under $200 or $300. Some clinics or family planning agencies offer abortions at minimal cost or even free of charge.

### Choosing the "Best" Method of Birth Control

Any individuals or couples who expect to have sexual intercourse should carefully consider the various methods of birth control and decide which seem most suitable and available to them. Birth control is not the responsibility of *just* the man or *just* the woman, but of *both partners*. A sexual encounter in which both partners assume that the other has provided for birth control, without any discussion, is an irresponsible encounter. If one partner lies about being protected by birth control, irresponsible exploitation is occurring. It should be kept in mind, too, that more than one method of birth control may be used. The more methods employed, the greater the protection.

Young people often ask me what form of birth control would be the most effective for them. Actually, most contraceptive methods are quite effective when used *correctly* and *consistently*. The important thing is to learn as much as possible about the positive and negative features of each method, and then to choose the method that seems to suit one's needs and sexual life-style best. Most types of birth control have potential risks and dangers, and all of them have their inconvenient features. Some feminists discourage the use of "non-natural" forms of contraception that introduce hormones or chemicals into the woman's body, while medical groups counter that the protective benefits of these methods outweigh the risks. It is essential for any couple to choose a method with which both partners feel comfortable, that both understand, and that they both can commit themselves to using *every* time they share sex. It is also important to remember that couples may use more than one form of birth control during the course of their relationship.

The laws of different states vary concerning the age at which a person may obtain birth control materials. Your local Planned Parenthood or Family Planning agency can provide you with appropriate information concerning your state. These organizations are often best equipped to give complete education about the various contraceptive methods, and then help in the decision making process. They can also often provide counseling help for people attempting to make decisions about sex or unwanted pregnancy. For more information on your local agencies, look in your telephone directory or write to one of the organizations listed in Appendix II.

### A Final Note on Parenthood

Teenage mothers and fathers often face serious problems. They may be treated unfairly by parents, friends, schools, and society. They often feel guilty and afraid as they face the confusion of deciding what to do. Some communities have special programs and counseling available for teenage mothers and fathers. Planned Parenthood and Family Planning agencies may be able to provide further information.

It must also be kept in mind that the world is facing the crunch of over-population. In underdeveloped countries, this

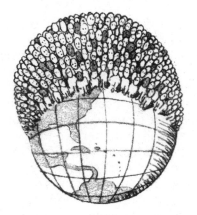

problem leads to disease, misery, and starvation, but over-population is very much a problem in the more developed, industrialized countries of the world too. Every new child in developed countries uses massive amounts of food and resources and contributes vast amounts of garbage to our pollution problems.

The earth's population grows at an astounding rate. Its first billion living inhabitants were not acquired until 1830. By 1960, the earth's population had reached three billion. At this rate, the earth could have six to ten *billion* living inhabitants soon after the year 2,000. Population experts and other scientists agree that this growing number of people could have disastrous effects for all of us, as we get low on food and sources of energy and high on pollution.

This represents simply another reason why sex—and its role in reproduction—carries with it important responsibilities. Our sexual feelings can provide us with the utmost pleasure and fulfillment. Yet, seeking the gratification of sex must mean paying attention to our responsibilities—to ourselves, our sexual partners, and our world.

### For Further Exploration
1. Parenthood.

a. On a separate paper, make a list of the qualities you feel are important for good parents to have. Take into consideration such things as the kind of relationship they have as a couple and with their children; financial security; personal characteristics;

abilities for communication; age; level of maturity; and emotional stability.

b. Now go back and carefully consider the list you made in (a) above. How would you rate yourself in each of the qualities you have listed? It might help to rate each quality with a number from the following scale:

| 1. | 2. | 3. | 4. |
|---|---|---|---|
| I have a long way to go | I'm getting closer all the time, but have plenty of time | Before long, I'll be there | I'm ready now on this score |

c. On a separate sheet of paper, make two columns with the following headings:

| (1) | (2) |
|---|---|
| Areas where my parents excelled, and where I want to be the same with my children: | Areas where my parents could have done better, and where I would like to be different with my children: |

Now, choosing from the following list, place items in the column where they fit best for you. Also, feel free to add your own items:

| | |
|---|---|
| Showing warmth and love<br>Trying to understand<br>Demonstrating trust<br>Setting good examples<br>Knowing when to compromise<br>Making fair rules<br>Being fair in enforcing rules<br>Giving the right amount of advice<br>Knowing when *not* to belittle<br>Providing security and stability | Teaching about sex<br>Showing and sharing inner feelings<br>Communication<br>Not judging too quickly<br>Allowing children's friends in the home<br>Giving a good allowance<br>Knowing when to show approval<br>Accepting differing values |

2.  Further research on conception, birth, and babies.
      a.  Using the books listed at the end of this chapter or refer-
ences you can find in a library, try to find more information on
the following subjects:
      — What happens when a sperm fertilizes an ovum?
      — What are the stages of growth that a fetus goes through
        during each week of its development?
      — What is "natural childbirth" and "Lamaze childbirth"?
      — How are identical twins formed, and how often do they
        occur?
      — Fertility drugs are sometimes used to help a woman be-
        come pregnant. How do these drugs work and why do
        they sometimes lead to multiple births—twins, triplets,
        or more?
      — What are all of the functions of the amnion, placenta, and
        umbilical cord?
      — Why is an incubator often used when a baby is born pre-
        maturely? What does the incubator do?
      b.  If you have never had much contact with babies during
their first few months of life, try to visit an infant day-care center
or to spend some time with a new mother. Try to get a better
idea of the amount of care required by a baby. After you have
had some time to think about your observations, make two lists:
1) The things you like *most* about babies and taking care of them;
2) The things that appeal to you *least* about babies and caring
for them.
3.  Birth Control
      a.  What information would you want to give these friends
of yours in the following situations? Remember, there are no pat
"right" or "wrong" ways to respond. Do what *you* think is best:
            (1)  A 16-year-old boy who is a friend of yours tells you
            that he and his girlfriend have had sexual intercourse
            several times. You inquire about the method of birth
            control they are using, and he tells you that they are
            just trying to be careful to avoid intercourse during the
            middle of the month.
            (2)  A 15-year-old girl you know has just discovered
            that she is pregnant, but she has not yet talked about

her problem with anyone. You are the first person she has told. She tells you that she wants to have an abortion but does not know how or where to obtain one.
(3) You are talking about birth control with a friend of your own sex and age. The friend insists that it is the girl's responsibility to use birth control since she is the one who gets pregnant. Your friend also believes that the particular method of birth control used is unimportant, saying "they all work if you use them right."

b. Do you think you would like to have children some day? If so, how many would you like to have? What are your reasons for thinking that this is your "ideal" family? Is the family larger or smaller than the family in which you were raised? What have you learned from the size of your family?

## For Further Reading

Bode, Janet. *Kids Having Kids: The Unwed Teenage Parent.* New York: Franklin Watts, 1980.

Brooks, Krail and DeWolf, Rose. *Changes: Becoming a Teenage Parent.* Philadelphia: Planned Parenthood of Southeastern Pennsylvania, 1979.

Carroll, L.; LaBelle, D.; Woolridge, V.; and Zarkowsky,L. *What Now? Under Eighteen and Pregnant.* Salem, MA (P.O. Box 2087): Origins, Inc.

Gordon, Sol and Wollin, Mina. *Parenting: A Guide for the Young.* New York: Sadlier/Oxford, 1975.

Lieberman, E. James and Peck, Ellen. *Sex and Birth Control: A Guide for the Young.* New York: Schocken Books, 1984.

National Alliance for Optional Parenthood. *Am I Parent Material?* Santa Cruz, CA (P.O. Box 8506): ETR Associates, 1977.

## More Nitty-Gritty

Even after reading the previous chapters in this book, there is a good chance you will still have some questions about human sexuality. New questions come to my mind often, and I sometimes have to search for a book or a person who can answer them.

In this chapter, I'll answer some of the questions that young people have often asked me but that are not discussed in detail in other sections of this book. If you have further questions not answered in this chapter, try looking up the topics in the index and finding information in earlier chapters. The references listed at the end of each chapter may also be good sources for further information.

The following questions and answers are grouped together according to their content:

### Questions About Personal Values and Sex

*Why don't parents talk to their kids more about sex?*
There are plenty of reasons. Parents often have difficulty seeing their children as sexual people and prefer to avoid the whole issue. Sometimes, parents put off talking about sex until they realize that their kids already know quite a bit about it; then they decide it won't be necessary to talk about sex at all. Some parents are just too embarrassed to deal

with sexual topics or feel that they do not have enough information themselves to be able to explain anything well. They may hope that the school will do something with sex education. There are even some adults who say that the less children are told about sex the better, somehow trying to believe that if kids don't learn about sex, they won't have sexual feelings or want to experiment with it. It should be kept in mind, however, that many people believe sex education to be one of the important responsibilities of parenthood. Of course, not discussing sex is a form of sex education too. It teaches that sex is something mysterious—perhaps even frightening or ugly—which should not be discussed. (See Chapter Six)

*How may a person overcome personal shyness toward sex and sexual activities?*
Shyness is not necessarily a bad thing, and some other people might find it quite appealing and appropriate. Although we live in times when people discuss sex more openly, boldness and aggressiveness regarding sex is a real turn-off for many. Nearly everyone is afraid and shy when they first start trying to establish loving relationships and when they first begin to explore sex. Often, much of the shyness disappears as confidence is gained. When shyness is considered to be a real problem by the individual, he or she might want to talk about it with a trusted friend or counselor (see Chapter Six). Among high school and college students, shyness is a common complaint.

*What has caused sex to be called dirty? Is sex really dirty or is it whatever people wish to make it?*
Our sex organs and sexual feelings are simply a part of human life. As civilized people began to realize the responsibilities and problems that go along with sex, rules, morals, and social attitudes began to develop. Different religions and cultures have very different values concerning the rights and wrongs of sexual behavior. The undercurrent of negative attitudes about sex in our culture—thinking of it as "dirty"—is largely the result of attitudes left over from pre-

vious periods in our history. The general feeling at that time was that sex should be used only to produce children and that sexual feelings and activity were mostly bad and disgusting. People were encouraged to deny and control their sexual feelings, often creating great guilt and conflict. Attitudes today are taking a less restrictive view of sex. However, more open sexual attitudes place more of the responsibility for careful decision-making on each of us as individuals.

*We always hear about boys trying to be seducers. Do girls ever set out to seduce?*

Seduction refers to an attempt at enticing a person into sexual activity. If one person seduces another through lies or trickery, that is irresponsible and exploitative (See Chapters Five and Seven). If both people are aware of what is happening and want to have sex, then it becomes a mutual seduction, and that may or may not be a responsible sexual encounter. In any case, seduction is often initiated by both males *and* females. It is also often done in irresponsible and exploitative ways by both males *and* females.

## Questions About the Body and Sex Organs

*Is it normal for one of a woman's breasts to be larger than the other?*

Many young women worry about their breasts. It is quite common for one breast to be slightly larger than the other. It is also typical for one breast to hang at a different position than the other. The great differences in women's breasts are largely the result of heredity and have nothing to do with how "sexy" a woman is. (See Chapter Two.)

*What is a hysterectomy? Can a woman still have sex after she has had a hysterectomy?*

A hysterectomy is a surgical procedure in which the woman's uterus is removed. Often, one or both of the ovaries are also removed. This surgery is done for a variety of reasons but especially when abnormal cells are detected indicating that the uterus is the site of a cancerous growth. Many physicians say it is wise for a woman to get the opinion of more than one doctor before agreeing to this surgery. In most hysterectomies, the vagina is not removed, although its position may be slightly different after the surgery. Women can still enjoy a full range of sexual activities following a hysterectomy, including intercourse. Of course, pregnancy is not a possibility after removal of the uterus.

*What is a Pap Test and what does a doctor do during an internal pelvic examination of a woman?*
For a Pap Test, a physician inserts a small instrument into the vagina and painlessly extracts some fluid and cells from the area of the cervix. A smear is made of this material on a glass slide and it is stained. Then, a trained specialist examines the smear under a microscope, looking for any abnormal cells that might indicate the beginning of disease, especially cancer. Girls and women should consider the Pap Test an essential part of regular physical examinations. For an internal, or pelvic, examination, a physician inserts two fingers into the vagina, using surgical gloves and a lubricant. By pushing gently against the uterus with these fingers and placing the other hand on the woman's abdomen, the physician can detect some abnormalities in shape or size of the uterus and ovaries. Some women worry that they will become sexually aroused by such an examination, but their worries are unfounded.

*Is an erection of the penis caused by the testes or by the mind?*
The testes produce male hormones that may have a minor effect on the male's interests and arousability for sex. The actual mechanism of penis erection is controlled largely by a spinal reflex. However, the mind (brain's cerebral cortex) has input too. Thinking about sex can stimulate an erection, just as fear or anxiety can make erection difficult. In men whose spinal cords have been severed so that there is no connection between the brain and the penis, erection can still occur because of the reflex. Many men who are paralyzed below their waists can still experience erection and participate in sexual activities. (See Chapter Two.)

*If a man has lost one testis, can he still have a normal sex life?*

In males who have only one testis, there is usually no effect on sexual feelings, sexual performance, or the ability to reproduce. Their bodies develop normally, they are sexually active, and they can produce children.

*Is there any way to make a penis larger than it is?*

No, nor is there any good reason for trying. A boy's penis reaches nearly its full growth by his later teenage years, but penis size has nothing to do with the amount of pleasure it can give him or a partner. Some devices are sold with advertising suggesting they might increase penis size. Such devices are ineffective, and may cause damage to the penis. Males' penises are found in a variety of sizes and shapes, all perfectly normal and functional, unless some disease has actually produced an abnormally small organ. (See Chapter Two.)

*During a physical examination of a male, why does the doctor feel behind the testes and ask the guy to cough?*

Anytime an internal organ pushes through a weakness in the surrounding muscles, it is called a hernia, or rupture. There is a particular kind of hernia in which a small section of intestine may protrude through the abdominal muscles and even move down into the scrotum at times. The doctor is pushing at the opening where such a hernia could be felt, and coughing would cause it to be even more evident. This type of hernia is not very common. When present, it may require some sort of medical treatment. Hernias have nothing in particular to do with sex, even though young people joke about them as if they did.

## Questions About Sexual Functioning

*At what age does sex start to interest boys and girls? How old should two people be before they engage in sexual activity?*

This varies a great deal with different individuals. Some boys and girls become interested in sex and have sexual feelings at quite young ages, while others may not have such interests until they are teenagers or even older. There is also no way of establishing an age when people are ready for sex. Again, that varies with individuals and their circumstances. Each person must decide what kinds of limits he or she wants to have for sexual activities, taking into consideration many factors of responsibility. Careful reading of this book—especially Chapters One-Five, Eight and Ten—can help you think about some of these factors.

*How much sex can you have when you're young without hurting yourself for later on in life? If you have too many orgasms when you're young, will it make you unable to have sex when you're 50 or older?*

Sex and orgasms are not "used up" after a certain limit of activity has been reached. The male body continues to produce semen into old age, and both women and men can still have orgasms when they are old. As a matter of fact, research shows that the more sexually active a person is in youth and middle age, the more active he or she will tend to be in older age. Different people differ in how often they desire sexual release, and their bodies adjust themselves to those needs, regardless of age.

*Do boys get sexually excited easier than girls?*

There is a great deal of controversy over this very question today. Traditionally, it had been assumed that boys become sexually aroused more quickly than girls and that boys' sexual interests were stronger. Current research is indicating that this is probably not true at all. Although sexual excitement in boys may be more noticeable because of erection of the penis, girls have the potential of becoming aroused just as rapidly and to as great an extent. It is certainly *not* true either that a girl can be expected to be in greater control of her sexual feelings and therefore should be the one to stop a sexual encounter before it "goes too far."

*I'm a girl, and I don't understand how an erect penis can ever fit into a vagina. Isn't the vagina too small?*

Many girls worry that a penis will never be able to fit into their vaginas. Actually, the walls of the vagina are very elastic and can accommodate even a very thick penis. (After all, the vagina can stretch to allow a large baby to be born.) During sexual excitement the vagina lengthens and widens somewhat, and the inner walls become slippery with lubrication. These changes help with accommodation of the penis. During early sexual contacts, plenty of time should be taken for insertion of the penis, to avoid any discomfort and to allow for proper lubrication. (See Chapter Two.)

*Why is it that a male sometimes can't keep his erection during sexual activity.*

When a male has difficulty maintaining the erection of his penis, professionals usually refer to the problem as *impotence*. Most males experience erection difficulties from time to time, often the result of fatigue, nervousness, depression, alcohol or drug consumption, or just not being especially excited sexually. It may be a signal of guilt about sex or some feelings that need to be talked over with his partner. Some men have trouble getting an erection when they feel pressured to perform well in sex and have some fear that they will not meet expectations. Occasional problems of this sort are best dealt with by accepting them without embarrassment or fear. If a problem remains for a long period of time, it may be wise to seek help from a qualified sex therapist. (See Chapter Seven.)

*How long does it take for an average person to reach a climax (orgasm) during sex?*

The length of time required to reach orgasm varies with the individual and the amount of stimulation. During sexual activity leading to orgasm, the majority of men reach climax within 4 minutes after entering the vagina. Some men may reach orgasm in a minute or less. However, it is possible for males to *learn* how to prolong the time it takes to reach orgasm, especially by careful attention to masturbating slowly and not allowing oneself to ejaculate. Yet, again there is much individual variation. Some women can reach orgasm a few seconds after beginning intense sexual activity; others might require a much longer time and more direct stimulation of the clitoris. (See Chapter Three.)

*Is it all right for a girl to engage in sex during her period?*
The menstrual cycle is a normal part of female life (see Chapter Two). Even during menstruation, or the "period," when a small amount of blood and other tissues seeps out of the vagina, there is no need to limit day-to-day activities or sexual activities. Some couples prefer not to have sexual contact during menstruation because of the blood present. However, there is no medical reason for this; neither partner can be harmed by sex during the period. It should be kept in mind that although the chance of pregnancy occurring is less during menstruation, *pregnancy can still occur.* (See Chapters Two and Ten.)

*Why is it that people sometimes feel guilty after having sex?*
People feel guilty whenever they do something that they think is wrong or that has hurt someone. When a sexual encounter leads to guilt, it may be the result of having learned that sex is wrong or bad in some way. It may also mean that before the individual engages in sexual activity again, he or she should think about it carefully and talk seriously about sex with others. Several exercises at the ends of chapters in this book may be able to help you think through your attitudes and values about sex.

*Can a doctor tell by any kind of examination whether or not you have had sexual activity?*
Generally speaking, no. There is no way of determining what kinds of sexual activities are being participated in by examining the penis, mouth, or throat. In the vagina and anus, the presence of sperm in a microscopic examination is an indication of sexual activity, but such an examination must take place within a few hours. Presence or absence of the hymen, is, of course, not an accurate indication. Presence of a sexually transmitted disease is a sign that some sort of sexual contact has taken place for both males and females.

## Questions About Other Sexual Activities
*Can a person go through life without any sex and still be happy? If you don't masturbate or have sexual intercourse, can you become physically ill?*

Having sexual feelings and needing to express them are important and normal parts of the human personality. Very few people go through life without having at least some outlets for their sexual drives. However, no physical damage is done by not participating in sexual activities. If an individual finds other outlets for the sexual energy he or she generates, then there might be no problems in avoiding sex and being happy. However, if lack of participation in sex results from fear, guilt, other negative attitudes about one's own sexuality, or inability to become involved with other people, emotional difficulties may develop which might require some discussion with a good counselor. (See Chapter Six.)

*Can masturbation cause any damage to physical or mental health?*
Masturbation is a harmless practice, not leading to any physical or mental damage. Even in those individuals who masturbate very often (several times a day), there seems to be no particular harm done. Masturbation is a normal way of expressing sexual feelings, and almost everyone masturbates at various times during his or her life. Of course, it is also all right to choose not to masturbate. (See Chapter Three.)

*If you participate in some homosexual acts or heterosexual acts at the age of 12 or 13, does it mean that you are going to be homosexual or heterosexual?*
Not at all. In fact, sexual contact between members of both sexes is very common in children and younger teenagers. Studies have shown that for boys under the age of 15, homosexual contact is more common than heterosexual, but most boys do not become homosexual. It is not unusual for two or more young people of either the same or opposite sexes to explore one another's bodies and experiment with sexual activities. To become sexually excited by such situations is no indication that a person is homosexual or heterosexual.

### Miscellaneous Sex Facts
*Is there such a thing as "Spanish Fly" and does it really get you sexually turned on? Do any foods or drugs enhance sexual performance?*

"Spanish Fly" is the slang name for cantharides, a chemical extracted from a European beetle that has been rumored to make people sexually excited. It is often talked about as a substance that is slipped into a person's drink or food so they will be easier to persuade into sex later, which is obviously an irresponsible, exploitive attitude. In fact, cantharides does not increase sexual desire and can be a dangerous chemical to take into the body, with serious—even deadly—side effects. Certain foods (olives, eggs, etc.) and drugs have also developed reputations as being aphrodisiacs—sexual stimulants. These are apparently myths. Although certain drugs, such as alcohol and marijuana, may lower sexual inhibitions, they apparently often hinder actual sexual performance.

*Can doctors tell before a baby is born whether it is a boy or a girl?*
Several tests have been developed to determine the sex of a child before birth, but most are not considered reliable. One method that can be used, but is generally not done unless there is a special medical problem, is examination of amniotic fluid. A long, hollow needle is inserted through the pregnant woman's abdomen into the amnion surrounding the fetus, and a small amount of fluid is withdrawn containing some cells from the fetus. Special techniques are then used to make the chromosomes in these cells visible. At that time the sex chromosomes can be observed and a determination made as to whether they are XX (a girl) or XY (a boy). Most physicians make no attempt to determine the sex of a child until it is born. (See Chapter Ten.)

*Can you get V.D. (STD) from dirty hands?*
No. You get V.D., now usually referred to as sexually transmitted diseases (STD), when a germ is transmitted to your body by an infected person, regardless of her or his degree of cleanliness or yours. Since STD germs can survive outside the body for only a very few seconds, they are almost always transmitted by direct body contact, especially when the sex organs are together. Cleanliness is no guarantee of protection against STDs. (See Chapter Seven.)

# Appendix I: Four-Letter and Other Words

Here is an alphabetical list of words that relate to human sexuality. Some slang terms are included—those terms sometimes called "dirty words." Although slang words may be offensive to some people, it seemed important to include some of them in this list, so their meanings and the more acceptable scientific terms can be learned. For some of the words, proper pronunciation is given.

More information on most terms may be found by consulting the index and finding the pages in the text where the words are used.

*Abortion*—the expulsion of an embryo or fetus from the uterus before birth.

*Adolescence*—a time of growth and change between childhood and adulthood.

*Adultery*—sexual intercourse which occurs between a married person and someone other than his or her spouse (husband or wife).

*AIDS*—an abbreviation for acquired immune deficiency syndrome, a serious disease that can be transmitted through sexual contact.

*Balling*—slang for sexual intercourse.

*Balls*—slang for testes.

*Beat-off* (or "Beat the Meat")—slang for masturbation, especially in males.

*Bisexual*—a person who is sexually attracted by and/or participates in sexual activity with members of both sexes.

*Box*—slang for vagina.

*Cervix* (SIR-vicks)—the narrow part of the female's uterus, or neck of the uterus, which extends into the vagina.

*Chancre* (SHANK-er)—a painless, oozing sore that appears in early syphilis, usually on the sex organs.

*Cherry*—slang for hymen.

*Chlamydia* (kla-MID-ee-uh)—a sexually transmitted disease that has become a national epidemic. It creates a variety of unpleasant symptoms and should be treated promptly.

*Circumcision* (sir-come-SIZ-zhun)—removal of the foreskin, or fold of skin which covers the end of a boy's penis. May also be done to expose the clitoris in females.

*Clap*—slang for gonorrhea.

*Climax*—see orgasm.

*Clitoris* (KLIT-or-iss)—a small organ located above the opening of the vagina in the female vulva; highly sensitive to sexual stimulation.

*Cock*—slang for penis.

*Coitus* (KOH-ih-tuss)—a scientific term for sexual intercourse.

*Come* (or cum)—slang for orgasm or for semen.

*Conception* (kun-SEP-shun)—see fertilization.

*Condom* (KON-dum)—a rubber or membrane sheath worn over the penis during sexual intercourse to collect semen, preventing pregnancy, and to prevent the spread of venereal diseases.

*Contraceptive* (kon-tra-SEP-tiv)—any device which prevents fertilization of an ovum by a sperm.

*Crabs*—slang term for sexually transmitted pubic lice that infect the pubic area, causing itching. They are highly contagious.

*Cunt*—slang for vagina.

*Diaphragm* (DI-uh-fram)—a rubber disc inserted into the vagina and over the cervix before intercourse to prevent sperm from entering the uterus.

*Dick* (or dink)—slang for penis.

*Dyke*—slang for lesbian or female homosexual; often used to offend or insult.

*Egg*—see ovum.

*Ejaculation* (ee-jack-u-LAY-shun)—the sudden emission of semen from the penis during male orgasm.

*Embryo* (EHM-bree-oh)—a developing organism. For the first 8 weeks of development in the uterus, a human being is called an embryo.

*Erection* (ee-RECK-shun)—the male's penis becoming filled with blood, so that it becomes longer, thicker, harder, and stiffer.

*Erotic* (ee-ROT-ick)—anything having to do with sexual love and sexual feelings.

*Exhibitionist*—an individual who gains sexual excitement from exposing the sex organs.

*Faggot*—slang for male homosexual; often used to offend or insult.

*Fallopian tube* (fah-LOPE-ee-an)—a hollow tube leading from the ovaries to the uterus. Fertilization usually takes place while the ovum is in this tube.

*Fertilization*—a sperm entering an ovum, combining the chromosomes.

*Fetus* (FEE-tuss)—the developing infant inside the female's uterus from 8 weeks until birth.

*Foreplay*—sexual petting which eventually leads to more intensive sexual activity such as intercourse.

*Foreskin*—the fold of skin which covers the head of the boy's penis at birth. The head, or glans penis, is exposed by pulling the foreskin back.

*Fuck*—slang for sexual intercourse, although the term is used in a wide variety of ways currently.

*Gay*—slang for homosexual or bisexual; preferred by most homosexual men, while most homosexual women prefer to be called "lesbians."

*Gonad*—biological term for a sex gland, either ovaries or testes.

*Gonorrhea* (gone-or-REE-uh)—a sexually transmitted disease often characterized by a burning feeling during urination and discharge of pus from the urethra.

*Hard-on*—slang for erection.

*Herpes* (HER-peez)—a viral sexually transmitted disease characterized by painful blisters that may recur.

*Heterosexual*—anything applying to the opposite sex.

*Homo*—slang for homosexual; often used to offend or insult.

*Homosexual*—anything applying to the same sex. More specifically, an individual who is sexually attracted primarily to others of his or her own sex.

*Hormones*—chemicals produced by endocrine glands (including the ovaries and testes) which help regulate body activities.

*Horny*—slang for sexually aroused or being interested in sex.

*Hymen* (HI-mun)—fold of skin which often partially covers the opening to the vagina in girls, until it has been broken in some way.

*Impotence* (IM-poh-tense)—inability in a male to achieve or maintain an erection for sexual activity.

*Incest*—sexual activity between closely related individuals.

*Intercourse*—see sexual intercourse.

*I.U.D.* (or Intrauterine Device)—a birth control device inserted into the woman's uterus to prevent pregnancy.

*Jack-off* (or Jerk-off)—slang for masturbation.

*Labia* (LAY-bee-uh)—the "lips" in the female's vulva area which cover the opening to the vagina.

*Lesbian* (LEZ-bee-un)—another term for a female homosexual.

*Masturbation* (mass-ter-BAY-shun)—stimulating one's own sex organs, often with the hands, to produce sexual excitement and often orgasm.

*Menopause*—the time in a woman's life when she has completely stopped having menstrual periods.

*Menstruation* (men-stroo-AY-shun)—stage of the female menstrual cycle in which some inner lining of the uterus, along with a small amount of blood leaves the body through the vagina.

*Mons* (mahnz)—the small mound of tissue, covered with hair in adults, just above the sex organs.

*Natural Family Planning/Fertility Awareness*—an approach to birth control that combines charting the menstrual cycle, daily temperature checks, and regular checking of the woman's cervical mucus. If carefully and consistently used, it is an effective strategy for birth control or for determining the best time to get pregnant.

*Nocturnal emission*—ejaculation of semen from a male's penis while he is asleep.

*Nuts*—slang for testes.

*Orgasm* (OR-gaz-um)—the pleasurable climax which releases tension after it has built up as sexual excitement.

*Ovary*—two glands in the female, located near the uterus, which produce female hormones and ova.

*Oviduct*—see Fallopian tube.

*Ovulation* (oh-view-LAY-shun)—the time during the female's

menstrual cycle when the ovum ruptures through the ovary wall and begins its journey to the fallopian tube.

*Ovum* (plural: ova)—the egg, produced by the female, which when fertilized by a male's sperm develops into a new human being.

*Penis* (PEE-niss)—the sex organ of the male, which becomes erect during sexual excitement. It carries both urine and semen to the outside of the male's body.

*Petting*—any touching of sex organs or breasts other than intercourse.

*Pornography*—pictures or written material of a sexual nature, which stimulate thinking about sex and sexual arousal.

*Premature ejaculation*—a difficulty in which the male reaches orgasm too soon for either his own or his partner's enjoyment; also called lack of ejaculatory control.

*Prepuce* (PREE-poose)—another scientific term for foreskin.

*Prick*—slang for penis.

*Prostitute*—an individual who participates in sexual activity for money.

*Puberty*—the time in a person's life when the sex organs become capable of reproduction.

*Pubic hair* (PYOU-bick)—the coarse, curly hair which surrounds the sex organs in older adolescence and adulthood.

*Pussy*—slang for vagina or vulva.

*Queer*—slang for homosexual, often an insulting or offensive term.

*Rape*—forcing a person to participate in sexual activity against her or his will.

*Rubber*—slang for condom.

*Rub-off*—slang for masturbation in females.

*Sado-masochist* (SAY-do-MASS-oh-kist)—an individual who gains sexual pleasure by inflicting or receiving pain or humiliation.

*Safe*—slang for condom.

*Sanitary Napkin*—an absorbent pad used by females to absorb the menstrual flow during menstruation.

*Screwing*—slang for sexual intercourse.

*Scrotum*—the pouch of skin in which the male's testes are contained, below the penis.

*Semen* (SEE-men)—the thick, sticky fluid which contains sperm, ejaculated by the male from the penis during orgasm.

*Sexual Intercourse*—the erect penis of the male entering the vagina of the female.

*Sexually Transmitted Diseases* (STDs)—those infections whose germs are spread from person to person by close body contact, usually sexual; also formerly called venereal diseases.

*Snatch*—slang for vagina.

*Sperm*—the microscopic cells produced by the male's testes which can fertilize the female's ovum.

*Sterilization*—any procedure which causes a male or female to be unable to reproduce by not allowing the sperm or egg to be present for fertilization.

*Syphilis* (SIFF-ill-is)—a dangerous sexually transmitted disease characterized by three stages.

*Tampon*—a cylinder of absorbent material inserted into the vagina to absorb the menstrual flow during menstruation.

*Testes* (TESS-teez) (Singular: testis)—two glands in the male, located in the scrotum, which produce male hormones and sperm.

*Transsexual*—an individual who feels trapped in a body of the wrong sex, and strongly wants to have a body of the opposite sex.

*Transvestite*—a person who gets sexual or other gratification from dressing in clothes usually worn by members of the opposite sex.

*Umbilical Cord*—the cord which attaches a developing fetus to the placenta, transferring food and oxygen to the fetus and waste products to the placenta.

*Uterus* (YOU-ter-us)—the female reproductive organ in which the fertilized ovum becomes implanted and grows for nine months into a baby.

*Vagina* (vuh-GINE-uh)—the elastic muscular canal extending down from the uterus to an opening in the vulva. It becomes lubricated during sexual arousal.

*Vasectomy*—a surgical procedure in which a male's sperm ducts (vas deferens) are cut, rendering him sterile.

*Venereal Diseases* (vehn-IHR-ee-al) (VD)—several diseases which are transmitted by close body contact, usually sexual;

now usually called sexually transmitted diseases (STD).

*Virgin*—a person who has never experienced sexual intercourse.

*Voyeur*—an individual who seeks sexual excitement by peeking in windows or other means to see people nude or involved in sex.

*Vulva*—the external sex organs of the female.

*Wet dream*—slang for nocturnal emission.

*Whack-off*—slang for masturbation.

*Womb (woom)*—another name for the uterus.

# Appendix II: Organizations That Can Provide Information and Help

**About Sexuality, Sex Education, and Family Life**

Sex Information and Education Council of the U.S. (SIECUS)
80 Fifth Avenue—Suite 801-2
New York, New York 10011
    Telephone: (212) 929-2300

American Association of Sex Educators, Counselors, and
    Therapists (AASECT)
Eleven Dupont Circle, N.W.—Suite 220
Washington, D.C. 20036
    Telephone: (202) 462-1171

Community Sex Information, Inc.
    (Provides sex information by telephone during evening
    hours)
    Telephone: (212) 982-0052

Los Angeles Sex Information Helpline
    (Telephone information during evening hours)
    Telephone: (213) 653-1123

Kinsey Institute for Sex Research, Inc.
    Room 416, Morrison Hall
    Indiana University
    Bloomington, Indiana 47401

## About Birth Control and Family Planning

Your local Planned Parenthood or Family Planning Agency
(See your telephone directory and local advertising)

Planned Parenthood Federation of America, Inc.
810 7th Avenue
New York, New York 10019
(Can provide a list of local Planned Parenthood affiliates.)

Alan Guttmacher Institute
111 Fifth Avenue
New York, New York 10011

Zero Population Growth
1601 Connecticut Avenue, N.W.
Washington, D.C. 20036

## About Sexually Transmitted Diseases

VD National Hotline
National toll-free telephone (for anywhere in U.S.A.):
1-800-227-8922
Telephone in California: 1-800-982-5883
Call for STD information or referral to local clinics for
treatment. Hours: 8 am–8 pm (PST) weekdays.

Public Health Service AIDS Hotline: 1-800-447-AIDS

## About Homosexuality

Homosexual Community Counseling Center
30 East 60th Street, #803
New York, New York 10022

National Gay Task Force
80 Fifth Avenue—Room 1601
New York, New York 10011

Gay and Lesbian Community Services Center
1213 North Highland Avenue
Hollywood, California 90038

# Index

Page numbers in *Italics* indicate a diagram on the page. Also consult Appendix I, *Four Letter and other Words*, pages 180–186.

# About the Author

Gary K. Kelly has been working with young people throughout his professional career as an educator and counselor. He is Headmaster of The Clarkson School and Director of the Student Development Center at Clarkson University in Potsdam, New York. He is certified as a Sex Educator and as a Sex Therapist by the American Association of Sex Educators, Counselors, and Therapists, and has served as Editor of the *Journal of Sex Education and Therapy* since 1982. Kelly is a frequent consultant and conference speaker in the field of human sexuality. In addition to this book, he has authored a college textbook on sexuality, a book on male sexuality, and numerous articles for professional journals. He lives outside of Potsdam, New York with his wife Betsy and two daughters, Casey and Chelsea.